MARGARET HAUGHERY

Bread Woman of New Orleans

Margaret Haughery

Bread Woman of New Orleans

By
Flora Strousse

Illustrated by Lili Réthi

HILLSIDE EDUCATION

Cover and interior book design by Mary Jo Loboda

Cover image: *Portrait of Margaret Haughery* (detail) by Jacques Amans,
New Orleans, c. 1842, courtesy wikimedia

ISBN:978-0-9976647-5-1

Hillside Education
475 Bidwell Hill Road
Lake Ariel, PA 18436
www.hillsideeducation.com

CONTENTS

1

JUST KEEPS ROLLIN' ALONG

No one on the boat could have suspected that the Haugherys were honeymooners. Unlike most on their wedding trip, this couple had an air of anxiety; yet, their shy glances left no doubt of deep love between them.

The young husband, pale and often listless, gazed at his wife with eyes set deep in their sockets and gleaming with unnatural brilliance. They had gone to their stateroom after the noonday meal, and he apologetically said, "If you don't mind, Margaret, I think I'll be taking a little rest."

"And why should I mind?" his wife asked cheerily. "Sure rest is the medicine that will bring you back to health."

Charles stretched himself out on the bunk, and his wife, always careful not to alarm him, passed her hand fleetingly across his forehead. As she had suspected, he was feverish again, but Margaret tilted her tones to a high cheerful pitch when she added, "I'll be taking a little look around the boat, and later you will join me for a walk."

"That I will, darling," Charles promised wearily.

It was the weariness in his voice that wrung her heart, her husband's pathetic effort to pretend he was well when both knew their southward journey had been held out by the doctors as only a slim chance for Charles's recovery. Margaret quietly closed the stateroom door and moved down the long dim corridor. At the end, a gray shaft of light suggested the sun might be shining; in the dreary long passageway it was difficult to tell. She moved swiftly on, head erect, her gait revealing unusual strength and resolution for a young woman of twenty-two.

The boat they traveled was *The Hyperion,* which, though not lavish as some of the floating palaces soon to make their way down the Mississippi, seemed very splendid to Margaret—splendid and gay, gaudy and a bit confusing. She had found a small alcove at the aft of the ship, outside the large lounge. It was protected from too much wind and sun, and she and Charles often sat there watching the trail of water churned up by the paddle wheel, water brown as a bitter brew of coffee. Margaret thought to go there then, but after reaching the vast interior—much like an enormous ballroom vaguely divided with wooden latticework—she decided to linger for a while. Though shy, she was vitally interested in all kinds of people, and those sailing down the Mississippi in 1835 were as varied as their many tongues and dialects.

Only thirty years before, the American representative had received the keys of New Orleans from the Spaniards, and Louisiana was formally transferred to the United States. This astonishing purchase had as yet scarcely affected the Creoles, those first settlers from France and Spain whose most prized memories were of glittering courts and monarchs.

Less real than their dreams was the fact that their state was now annexed to the United States! Indeed, to the Creole most newcomers were untutored barbarians, whom they preferred to identify only with rough boisterous river-men. For their part, the Americans, who during the past five years had come to New Orleans in great numbers, termed the Creoles "decadent foreigners" and were gaining ascendency over them. The whole world of prejudice and snobbery was confined within the limits of the boat.

The largest section of the lounge was the dining area. A group of Creoles still lingered at a table, chatting in French and letting out ripples of laughter when a *bon mot* was supplied by one of their party. The Creole women were extremely beautiful, lavishly dressed and jeweled, their flawless, slender fingers suggesting lives of languor and ease. Even the Creole men—more poised and better mannered than the Americans—had an air of foreignness, as if they had been molded to pursue poetry, art or music, rather than the more rugged professions.

Margaret, whose life had been full of toil and sadness, found these people who fluttered like exotic birds pleasurable to watch. Though scarcely noticing the prosperous Americans aboard, the "foreigners" seemed more kindly to their servants, more responsive to beauty than those of Anglo-Saxon strain.

Margaret, who held staunchly to the rule of judging no one but herself, was often the recipient of a pleasant word, an inquiry about her husband's health from the Creole women. Though she dressed with utter simplicity, perhaps the sparkle in Margaret's eyes and her general cast of feature revealed her Gaelic strain, which diluted discipline with warmth, humor and wit. The Irish were not ashamed to show their feelings, and she—whose maiden name was Gaffney—was Irish to the core.

Sometimes, when she heard the Creole ladies mention family connections with the French and Spanish courts, she wondered wryly if the name O'Rourke would ring in their ears as merely another Irish immigrant. For Margaret's own mother was a lineal descendant of the great house of O'Rourke, Prince of Breffny, one of the most courageous chieftains ever to battle the British foe. Although those early intrepid noblemen had long been banished, time had been powerless to extinguish in the Irish people their flaming love of freedom.

After Margaret tarried for a while, thinking her private thoughts, she decided to take a turn around the deck. She breathed in deeply as she hurried on, and, rounding a corner, almost collided with another woman. So austere and reproachful was this stranger that Margaret hastened to apologize.

"I'm sorry," she said. "So deep I was in thought, as not to be noticing—"

"That's quite all right," the woman said. She seemed unable to conceal her real cause for displeasure, and added, "It's a disgrace the way those people behave." The stranger gestured toward a window where the Creoles still sat sipping their brandy, laughing, telling jokes. Her gaze then wandered back to Margaret's simple dress, and she nodded in approval. "I'm sure a sensible woman like you must find these creatures distasteful," she added sternly. Then she moved to Margaret's side and gestured that they should walk along together, while she awaited some reply.

"It's not for me to be judging," Margaret said. "For myself, I've always felt others must decide what they want according to their consciences."

"But those—those people give themselves such airs," the woman went on. "And wouldn't you think they'd let go their foreign ways and learn to speak English?"

The stranger continued to express her displeasure for all foreignness, finally taking a dig at the Irish. She termed them a low-class breed of ruffians, brawling and drinking and swearing all over the place—and if the influx of Catholics into America did not soon cease the Jesuits would soon be taking over the country and a Pope installed in Washington.

"Of course," she went on, "it's worse in New Orleans. But since the Louisiana Purchase, more and more patriotic, red-blooded Americans are coming. Just you wait, they'll put things aright."

"Is it your idea, then, that those of Catholic faith are not good Americans?" Margaret asked with feigned innocence. "If so, you're speaking to one who definitely disapproves this shallow view."

"Oh, I *am* sorry," the woman replied. "I was not talking about people like *you*. It's quite obvious you're a lady. But if you could see those Paddies, those roughnecks digging the canal, those petty shopkeepers fighting and drinking and making trouble, I'm sure you would agree with me."

"That's no more than I am, myself," Margaret returned. "Indeed, I'm not positive if after digging a dirty canal, I might not also find a few nips very welcome. Did you ever think of it that way?"

"No," the woman said, she never did.

And Margaret, drawing herself up with a hauteur of an O'Rourke princess, put in proudly, "If you'll excuse me now, I'd rather be walking by myself."

She started on ahead of the woman and decided to go to

the stateroom to see if her husband had awakened. He had, and seemed to be feeling better since his nap.

Margaret told him about her visit to the lounge, her interest in the Creoles whose gay carefree manner suggested that time is only meant to kill. She did not, however, mention the woman who had joined her—because, since Charles's illness, any slight or hostile attitude increased his hankering to go home. For him home was Ireland, which in memory had to him become a haven of tranquillity. In truth, Charles had known only hardship in his youth, so that faraway place must have become a symbol of his yearning to return again to vigor and health.

"A breath of air will do you good, my darling," Margaret told him, "so let us first take a turn on the deck, then find our cozy nook."

Again she moved down the dim corridor, this time slowly, pacing her footsteps so that Charles would not lag behind. On the second deck, they crossed through the partition where gamblers endlessly sat around large tables, each seemingly assured that Lady Luck would smile on him.

The cards deftly shuffled and dealt revealed hands and sleeves reaching across the table that could be consulted as a sort of guide map of the human flow down the Mississippi. From beneath fabric of uncut velvet, white fingers unscarred by toil told of a Creole returning to his home in New Orleans; hands with greater strength, yet free from signs of menial work, suggested a rich planter who had come from the Carolinas with his slaves and his oxen to start anew and cultivate the soil in Natchez; sinewy, muscled fingers identified a young fellow as having previously manned a flatboat on the river. And, of course, there were the splashy fabrics of professional gamblers' sleeves, wherein were hidden an extra card or two!

As the Haugherys passed the players, Margaret noticed a large pile of money passed across the table. Such a sum would keep Charles and her in food and lodgings for at least a year! They strolled around the deck at a snail's pace, then settled in their usual alcove, which afforded privacy. There, away from the prying eyes of people, it was soothing to watch the trail of water and hear the constant churn of the whirling paddle. Sometimes from the first deck, where alongside the boiler room freight and cattle were kept, came the mournful cry of an animal bewailing its confinement.

They had left the frost behind and were nearing Natchez and would soon be in their future home in New Orleans.

"Before long, you'll be chipper as a squirrel," Margaret maintained cheerily. "See the fresh green foliage on that bank beyond; I'm sure there are flowers too."

Charles smiled and replied, "When you speak of green, it's Ireland I think of, Margaret. Sure, you have to admit this wide, muddy river is no match for the glorious Shannon."

"And, sure *you'll* have to admit we've never been persecuted for our Faith in America," she replied.

Margaret then remembered the snobbishness of the woman on her walk, and she had to admit that prejudice was not absent even in this great country of her choice. But, she thought, America was young, with the battle of 1812 not far behind. Natural that a country so recently shorn of shackles should have growing pains. If only Charles would come to love this land as much as she did!

As they sat holding hands, Margaret tried to encourage her husband, prayerfully hoping that some of her strength might be conveyed to him.

"You must *want* to get well," she said.

And Charles replied, "I do."

They lingered, and the skies which had been cloudless gradually paled into a gloomy gray. Winds, gathering in the Gulf of Mexico at almost hurricane speed, were starting to sweep northward, ruffling the river. Soon white foam transformed the Mississippi into a cauldron of bubbling, brownish water. After Charles and Margaret hurried into the lounge, a voice outside bellowed:

"Clear the decks! We are in for a big blow!"

The force of the gale increased until the steamboat bobbed like a cork on the choppy water. Paddle wheels seemed powerless against the current, but the alert captain of *The Hyperion* coaxed the boat slowly toward a bank. After nosing her into the mud, a red-faced, stalwart seaman jumped ashore and secured the vessel to a tree with a stout rope. All the while engines were kept running, so that the whirling blades prevented the boat from swerving sidewise to be grounded on the muddy shore.

Few people remained in the lounge, except those at the gambling tables, whose attention was so fixed upon the cards they seemed unaware of the storm outside. Although many of the passengers were ill, Charles was not affected and was extremely interested in the way the boat had been maneuvered to prevent the possibility of disaster.

"It was a feat well done! " he exclaimed.

His spirits were almost gay, as if the steering of the boat to safety was a symbol of his own future. Now he chatted about settling in New Orleans, where, in his present mood, life seemed to hold out great hope.

"And when I'm well again," he said, "I'll be finding work so that you can have a bit of leisure for a change."

That night Margaret tossed about in her bunk. The wind was still high and rain came down in sheets. She felt herself being taken back in time to another storm—this one at sea. She was a little girl of five, and though leaving Ireland had caused her parents sadness, they were also full of hope about settling in America. When Margaret asked why only she and a small brother had come, her father told her not to worry her pretty head—the others would be along after he had a home for the family and had earned enough money to pay for their fares. Though he'd seemed calm and assured, Margaret noticed that every time she mentioned her brothers and sisters left behind to her mother, she would turn her head away and cry; so the child had stopped asking.

That ship on which she came to America had huge sails and skimmed on the sea like a gull—until the time of the storm. Then, great swells swept over the deck, to recede with a sucking sound until another came and another— wild, fearsome waves, threatening to swallow up the boat. Curiously, she had never thought of that other storm at sea until now when past sensations were reproduced in the present, vividly recalling those early memories. Perhaps, Margaret thought, the reason for her forgetfulness of that voyage was because later events had to her been far more terrible. As a carefree child, she had not realized how close to complete destruction they had come on that voyage across the Atlantic.

Now, as an adult, it seemed almost miraculous that any of them had survived.

When the storm came those years ago, the captain had been forced to change his course, and for six long months the vessel had floundered in uncharted seas before finally reaching Chesapeake Bay. Rations had been reduced to one cracker a day. Thinking back, Margaret felt that her parents probably denied themselves even this scant fare so that their children might survive.

Seldom giving way to her emotions, she felt a rush of tears to her eyes. How happy and full of hope her parents had been when, with dangers left behind, they were secured at the pier in Baltimore! Uncertain of their destiny, the passengers had been drawn close together. Parting from those who had shared the dangers of the voyage was almost like wrenching family ties. This was especially true of one of their shipmates, Mrs. Richards, who, with her husband, was also going to make a home in Baltimore.

"Promise me," she implored the Gaffneys, "that we will keep in touch with one another."

Promises had been made. And, indeed, this woman's affection for little Margaret was soon after to provide a haven, which had it been denied, would have left a small child desolate and alone. Because, in 1822, scarcely three years after their arrival in America, an epidemic of yellow fever raged in Baltimore. Both of Margaret's parents and younger brother became infected with the plague and died within a week.

Now, Margaret, wide-eyed in her bunk, felt again the same rush of anguish and fear, as had that lonely little girl who suddenly found herself without a family. But Mrs. Richards had come, and they had clung together, weeping, because the woman had also lost her husband in the plague.

"You must be my little girl." Margaret could still hear her foster mother's voice.

What warmth it had been to know that she was wanted. And how clearly the finger of God had pointed the way! Because Mrs. Richards, though herself a Protestant, had kept an unspoken pact with the child's dead parents, and urged their daughter to cling to her own faith. The shock and bewilderment of that little girl had also been softened by her Jesuit confessor, Father McElroy, through whose wise counsel she had come to know that suffering is a part of the heavenly Father's plan.

And now on her way to New Orleans with her husband Margaret prayed fervently for grace to accept whatever might lie ahead. Briefly, then, she felt a wave of panic, because she loved Charles and, dear God, did not want to lose him like the others.

Her husband was stirring in his bunk.

"Charles, how do you feel, darling?"

"I'm feeling calm and fit this night," he said.

The rain had slackened and the wind lost its strength. Amid shouts from the sailors, she could feel the boat slide off its muddy anchorage, turn and renew its way down river.

Just before sleep came, she felt a new surge of gratitude to Mrs. Richards, who, although not warm and affectionate like her own mother, had always been fair. Well disciplined herself, she had made Margaret work hard, taught her many things she would need to know in the rugged life ahead. What if Mrs. Richards had been like that woman on the deck, and not allowed her charge to go to her own church! Then she would have never known Father McElroy, nor even met her husband. For, it was the good pastor who'd introduced them. He—

Margaret fell asleep.

The following days were so crystal clear that even the flowers could be seen along the shore line. The boat skimmed past large white-columned plantation houses, with cabins for the slaves trailing behind like miniatures in cardboard. Orange groves, fields of sugar and cotton, slender stalks of corn thrived in abundance, showing that these vast estates were carefully tended. South of Baton Rouge, levees had been thrown up along the shores.

Many people on the boat were busy packing, but the Haugherys had so little to stow away they remained at the rail excitedly watching the scenery. Soon their destination would be reached.

As they came close to New Orleans, they saw ships moored to heavy timbers along the shore. Blunt-bowed trading brigs from Europe lay alongside coasting craft from New England, New York, and Baltimore and Philadelphia. Negroes busily hauled precious burdens of furniture, woolen goods, farming implements and crude machinery from off the fleet of flatboats. *The Hyperion* docked alongside another steamboat about to take off and make its way up river.

Two modest pieces of luggage in hand, Margaret and Charles moved down the gangplank into a bedlam of bustle and sound. English, Spanish, French and German came from the lips of passengers and those who had come to greet them. The Negroes shouted and sang as they rolled hogsheads and hauled bales of cotton, their bodies drenched with sweat. There, in the low-lying delta land, humidity added to the heat resulted in a feeling of oppression.

Margaret, noticing Charles was pale, guided him and followed the other passengers until they reached an ill-paved muddy street. There the two stood, confused and uncertain, until a neatly dressed woman came up to them and said, "You must be the Haugherys. Father Mullon sent me down to meet you. He had a letter from your pastor in Baltimore,

Margaret and Charles moved down the ganplank into a bedlam of busle and sound

and has taken temporary lodgings for you, knowing you would be tired."

The kindly faced stranger glanced in a sympathetic way at Charles, suggesting that she had been informed about his illness.

Margaret, also glancing at her husband, was alarmed at his heightened pallor. He suddenly started to cough, and mopping his lips left a streak of bright red on his handkerchief. Margaret hastily thanked the woman, who led the way to a waiting carriage.

2

MAY I COME IN?

What a relief it was to have some place to go, instead of being forced to search about for rooms! Margaret breathed a sigh of gratitude that Father McElroy had let their plight be known, and for Father Mullon's thoughtfulness in securing a place where they could stay. They were driven to a small house on the downtown side of the city near Camp Street, in the parish of St. Patrick's where Father Mullon was the pastor. The Haugherys' quarters consisted of two small rooms in the rear of a plaster and wooden house. Outside the tiny area containing the cookstove and pantry shelves lay a garden. What a boon this spot of green would be, Margaret thought.

The garden did prove a haven in the year to come, because neither she nor Charles ever left the place except to go to the modest frame church. They did occasionally have visitors, friendly neighbors, and Father Mullon, who took time from his busy schedule to help the unfortunate Haugherys. For dreams of a happy future dimmed as time went by. Instead of improving, Charles' health worsened rapidly. He came to speak only of faraway Ireland, where, if he could but again gaze upon the patchwork of varied greens, lie beside the crystal waters of her lakes, surely, surely he could be well again.

Margaret was frantic, for she came to know that the whole venture in New Orleans had been most ill-advised. Even in winter, the weather there had little healing quality, especially for one with infected lungs. Although she was expecting a child, she would gladly have returned to Ireland with her husband. But when she suggested such a course, Charles became so agitated she let the matter drop.

That was not what he wished, he told her. She must remain in New Orleans while he went in search of health. After his recovery, he would return and provide for his wife and the child to come. Margaret discussed this idea with her pastor who urged that she remain patient until the babe was born. Then, if her husband had not put aside his yearning to see Ireland again, he must be allowed to take the trip.

Never in all her life would Margaret know deeper joy than with her suckling infant. The wee colleen, whom they christened Frances, was frail—but she, the mother, would nurse her to health. Although Charles seemed interested in their baby girl, she had not the power to turn him from his idea that only a trip to Ireland would make him a fit father. Although her heart was torn, Margaret decided there was nothing to do but let her husband go.

"I'll be back, darling," he promised her on the pier.

And, she, still forcing cheerfulness, replied, "I'm sure you will, my love."

Charles, however, did not return. Several months after his leaving, Margaret had a letter telling that her husband had died soon after reaching Ireland.

She tended little Frances with the fierceness of a lioness for her cub. All now between her and utter desolation was the fragile infant. Then, one day, Frances, restless even in sleep, could not be roused—and Margaret knew, even before she touched the tiny waxen fingers, that her baby was dead. For hours, unseeing, she rocked the lifeless figure, a question framing in her mind, "Where could she turn now?"

This was as close as Margaret had ever come, or ever would come to doubting her true Source of comfort.

Numbed by her sorrow, at first Margaret felt life held little in store. What brought her out of this state of listlessness, was a sense of duty toward others. For it suddenly came to her, that all during Charles's illness and before her child was born, she had been beholden to others. She no longer needed help. Strong and accustomed to toil, Margaret decided to seek employment so that she could now be the giver. Because, she thought, only through service would the awful anguish of her recent loss be lessened. And prayer! After that first moment of knowing not where to turn, she again found great comfort in prayer.

Margaret sought advice about possible employment from many of the parishioners who had been so kind to her. All of them tried to dissuade her from going to work so soon, so she decided to wait a few months until the opening of the new St. Charles Hotel where she had been promised a position. It was during those days of inactivity, that she learned something about New Orleans and of how a duel was used to precipitate a crisis in the city.

Although dueling was prohibited by law, actually such contests were so fashionable, so inevitable in New Orleans, that many fencing masters made great fortunes. Swordplay had been practiced in New Orleans since the beginning of the colony, but at this time, "avenging one's honor" were words frequently heard on the lips of young Creole men plentifully supplied with money. Plantations were flourishing and often the sons of the owners were sent abroad to be educated — usually in Paris. There, they studied, gambled, fought, and flirted with women. Back in their native state, these impetuous young blades often found release from boredom in the duel. Though the thrust of his blade could also kill when fighting a "duello," such affairs were conducted with the courtly manners of gentlemen.

Although Margaret had always worked hard, she had been shielded from the more worldly aspects of life. She was amazed, then, to learn of the "dueling oaks," a grove of extremely large trees, set on the outskirts of the city. She was told about them by a fellow parishioner at St. Patrick's who had come to take her for a drive.

"And why," asked Margaret innocently, "should grown men be settling their scraps with swords and pistols? Couldn't they talk things out sensibly?"

Her guest laughed and quoted a journalist of the time: "The least breach of etiquette, the most venial sin against politeness, the least suspicion thrown out of unfair dealing, even a bit of awkwardness, are causes sufficient for a cartel [duel], which none dares refuse."

Margaret's comment was, "Just foolishness," but since they were driving out, she said, she might as well have a look at the oaks.

This was the first time Margaret had a chance to see how differences between the old culture of the Creoles and the new vigor of Americans determined the face of a city. Instead of the usually accepted function of a thoroughfare, Canal Street was the boundary between two worlds. The portion lying north, was paradoxically called, "the downtown section of the city." Here the early settlers, first French then Spanish, and after intermarriage called Creoles, clannishly clung to ancient dreams. Even their courtyards seemed to conspire against prying eyes and concealed their interior beauties from the outside world. In contrast, the rich newcomers in the "uptown section" were only too eager to show what could be done with a little red-blooded initiative, and their velvety lawns and well-tended gardens were fully exposed to view.

The drive to the oaks took Margaret and her friend far beyond the city boundaries, because, although dueling was known to be a common practice, it was nonetheless against the law. Thus, the site selected for avenging affairs of honor was remote—and mysteriously beautiful as well. The enormous live oaks gave a sense of secrecy, their gnarled branches held high and letting down a spider-web cascade of Spanish moss. It seemed appropriate that the trees there should be shrouded.

After admiring the beautiful grove, Margaret said only perverse curiosity had lured her there, and happy she was that no contestants were present at the time.

Her friend explained that most duels took place early in the morning to insure secrecy from the law.

The following day, however, a duel did take place that became a matter of public concern and altered the future growth of the city. Within the grove of oaks, a young American was killed by a dashing Creole, a matter promptly passed on to the law. The survivor was placed on trial, and when he was acquitted, the Americans claimed justice had not been done and threatened reprisals. Determined to use this crisis as a means to further their own cause, an angry mob gathered around the house of the judge who had handed down the verdict, shouting that they had been insulted.

Cries went up in other parts of the city, and the State, not wanting further trouble, withdrew the city charter and issued another. This provided that New Orleans should be divided into three separate municipalities, each to be governed by a board of selected aldermen. A fourth board, constituting the City Council, was drafted from the three others and presided over by the mayor. Many of those problems of common interest to all were handled by the City Council. The first municipality embraced the Creole section, the second the American—or uptown section—the rest the city below Esplanade Avenue. Though the plan then seemed satisfactory to all, it would take more than arbitrary divisions to put down prejudice. In many ways, bigotry was again and again to rear its ugly head.

The new St. Charles Hotel opened its doors in 1837. Designed by Gallier and Dakin, two famous architects, the cost of construction was $800,000. Columns flanked the façade of the structure which was topped by a magnificent dome. The most splendid hotel in America, the St. Charles was considered one of the architectural wonders of the century. In New Orleans it was spoken of "as the parthenon is to Athens, Notre Dame to Paris and St. Mark to Venice."

It was little wonder, then, that when Margaret Haughery stepped across the threshold, wearing a simple dress and severe bonnet, she was awed by the elegance. She did not, however, enter through the wide, splendid front doors, but one at the rear leading to the servants' quarters. It bothered her not one jot that her status was that of a lowly laundress.

Her wages were adequate, and she had been promised that if her work proved satisfactory, added services would assure her higher pay. Besides, her room and meals were free so she could save most of her money for those who needed it more than she.

Meanwhile, Margaret decided she would scrub, rub and iron, so that her loneliness would find easement in sleep. It did not happen this way, because no matter how hard she worked, her aching arms were empty. Then Margaret came to know that she could only find forgetfulness through people.

In a small way this came to pass, because although quiet, Margaret's warmth drew people to her. She became the confidante of many of the servants, especially of a middle-aged chambermaid named Minna Weber whose family had come to America from Germany in 1726. She was an intelligent woman, and told Margaret many interesting historical facts about the Mississippi, mostly, of course, about her own early forebears.

Lured to Louisiana by false propaganda, thousands of Germans left their homes for America between the years of 1718 and 1724. Although some settled in New Orleans, most made their way to a place about twenty-five miles above the city. There, in a section still known as "the German Coast," those stalwart pioneers had transformed virgin forest into a liveable settlement.

"Yes," Minna would say proudly, "my grandfather hacked down the trees and built his home with his bare hands almost."

There were no plows, no horses, yet those hardy pioneers had managed to cultivate the soil. When Margaret's blue eyes glowed with admiration for such vigor, Minna would add, "There were leopards in the wilderness, bears, panthers, wildcats and snakes. And, ach, those savage Indians!" To burn down a village and scalp their victims was common practice.

Minna told how her own daughter, Gertrud, had come to New Orleans. Blond, slim, with breath-taking beauty— and also having the voice of an angel—Gertrud had been persuaded to sing *lieder* in a small, respectable cafe in the Creole section. There a fine young man of Spanish descent had fallen in love with her, and they were married. Though poor, they had been extremely happy—

At this point in her story, Minna's eyes swam with tears. Her daughter had died in childbirth, and—and— She could not go on.

The words were wrung from Margaret's lips: "What about the baby?"

"Oh, she is a *schöne madchen!*"

But, because the father had married again—a French woman who was not fond of Germans—Minna rarely saw her grandchild.

It was a shame, a pity she could not see the colleen, Margaret said, and was briefly tempted to tell about her own bereavement. But somehow, it seemed safer to contain her emotions behind sealed lips.

She had come to keep her troubles to herself and comfort others. Work, listen, sleep, and the most welcome, sleep. Then one night, when Margaret was less tired than usual, her attention was caught by the light in a window opposite her own.

The pale yellow circle sent out from a wick seemed to reveal in outline a large white bird. Astonished, Margaret dimmed the light on her own lamp and watched. Again this form appeared, but now clarified itself into the starched white headdress worn by a Sister of Charity. At the present angle, she could see the Sister gazing down, and Margaret was overwhelmed with curiosity as to why the woman's face was suffused with tenderness. The following day, she asked Minna whether the large house at the rear was a convent.

"No," Minna told her, "it's the Poyders Asylum."

"Asylum?"

"Yes. It's an orphanage put up by Mr. Poyders, and managed by some kind of nuns."

Minna went on to tell more about the man whose charity was known throughout the city. Margaret, however, had ceased to hear. But one word remained in her mind, "Orphans!" The mere thought of parentless children somehow brought a sense that her arms *need not be empty*.

She could scarcely wait until her afternoon off, when, as if drawn by a magnet, she hurried around the corner. Her timid knock was immediately rewarded by a door thrown open. There, on the threshold stood a young Sister with a group of poorly dressed, scrawny children clinging to her skirts.

Without shame, Margaret burst into tears.

"Please, Sister, may I come in?" she asked.

The astonished young novice told Margaret she should, indeed, come in. A stranger weeping bitterly at their door must have upset her, because she seemed a trifle nervous when she added, "I will go get Sister Regis *at once!*"

The pretty young nun's skirts swept the floor as she turned, some children still clinging to the billowing fabric. The others gazed silently at Margaret, as if puzzled as to why a grown-up woman wept. The youngsters were clean, but their hollow eyes and pallor suggested a deficiency in diet. Margaret's eyes rested on one little boy of about five, with sleek blond hair and a cowlick that defied the most vigorous brushing. Obviously, his clothes were hand-me-downs from an older boy, and, since there had been no time to alter them, hung on his small frame like a scarecrow's. Whatever misery he had known in the past, had in no way altered his pert, mischievous expression.

This boy moved closer to Margaret and asked, "What's your name, lady?"

"Margaret Haughery."

"I see—" Then he tried to repeat her name. "Margaret Ha-ah—what's the rest?"

"Just call me Margaret."

She decided then and there that if her last name was too difficult for children to pronounce, she would henceforth be known as just "Margaret."

"What is *your* name?" she asked.

He was close to her now and gazed at her with an air of solemnity.

"Paul," was his answer. Then, a small finger touched an unwiped tear on her cheek. "Why are you crying— does something hurt?"

She drew the little boy closer and said, "It did, but it doesn't hurt now."

The rustle of a skirt sounded from the corridor, and Sister Regis came into the room. Though her gait and manner had the resoluteness of one in authority, her face was extremely kind. She seemed about to tell the children to leave, but noting Margaret's arm around the boy, refrained from sending them away.

"Well, now," Sister Regis said, "how nice it is for you to visit us."

After that she glanced meaningfully at the hovering children. They knew at once that the look meant their

"What's your name, lady?" the boy asked, moving closer to Margaret

dismissal.

Paul disengaged himself from Margaret and said, "Maybe I'll see you again."

"I—I hope I may come again."

"I'm sure you will," Sister Regis said, and smiling gently at her visitor, added, "Now tell me all about it."

Again came a rush of tears, and Margaret could not speak, but Sister Regis showed no sign of surprise, only patience and understanding. When calmed, Margaret told the silent, listening woman about her recent sorrows, and of her own tragic childhood. Since she had learned of the existence of this home, however, she said, hope was again in her heart and a way had been pointed out for her future.

"I want to come and work for you and be with the children," she ended.

"You must consider well," Sister Regis told her. "We have no money to offer for services, indeed not enough for ourselves."

No, no! This was not what Margaret wanted. She had saved some funds of her own and when they were gone she would gladly beg if allowed to stay there and work. Please, please—?

"If this is how you feel," Sister Regis said, "it is providential all around." The superior explained then that it had but recently been decided that she, her Sisters and the children would withdraw from Poyders Asylum and form an institution of their own.

"Our funds are so meager," she went on, "it is practically impossible to find a suitable place. Perhaps you, who live in the world, would be better able—"

Margaret interrupted. "Oh, I will, I will. And, you can be assured, Sister, I'll not be sparing my legs to find a home for us."

When Sister Regis did not dispute the "us," Margaret

knew her offer had been accepted. What joy it would be to work with Sister Regis, for during their brief talk together she seemed indeed a sister, a mother, a friend! Yes, the first friend she had made in New Orleans to whom she could unburden her sorrow. And besides Sister Regis, there would also be the children!

"Do you have babies, too?" Asking this, Margaret's arms unconsciously rose in a cradling gesture.

"Indeed we do!"

Margaret decided to give notice at once at the hotel. In a week she would begin a new life of hope!

Her employers expressed regret when told that she was leaving. Might she not possibly reconsider and remain at a higher wage? Her look of radiance must have suggested a greatly improved status.

"It is not the pay," Margaret explained. "I simply have to go."

Only with Minna did she discuss her future plans, and German thrift prompted her friend to say that such a move was madness.

"You will have nothing for yourself. What about your future?"

Margaret laughed and told the anxious Minna that up to then there had seemed no future for her.

With dire clucking and reversion to guttural German phrases, Minna accepted her defeat with a fond "*auf Wiedersehen*."

3

TWO HAUNTED HOUSES

Resolute as a trooper, Margaret marched the streets of New Orleans, searching for a new home for the orphans. She forgot her shyness and reserve to inquire of strangers about possible vacant houses to be rented for practically nothing.

Meeting only with discouragement and aching feet, she decided as a last resort to visit a realtor. Since she had been told that such agents charged enormous fees, she was not very hopeful. To her astonishment, though, after being ushered into a grand office and giving a gentleman the reason for her visit, she was told quite matter-of-factly that there were two places which might suit her purpose.

When she timidly inquired about his fee, the gallant Creole told her that he, too, had the interest of orphans at heart. So if either of the houses met with her approval, he would waive his fee—he imagined both rentals would be comparatively low. Before Margaret had a chance to shower blessings on him, the man added, "I must tell you, though: no one else wants to live in either of these houses. They are supposed to be haunted."

If there was no more wrong with them than that, Margaret said spiritedly, the smiles of orphans and a sprinkling of holy water would fast remedy such a situation.

"You can't put fear in the heart of a woman who spent her first years chasing leprechauns," she added laughing.

One of these houses, the man went on to tell her, was as fine as any home on Royal Street. But perhaps, because of its unfortunate history, the owners might be willing to lease it reasonably. The other house—here he shuddered with distaste—was scarcely habitable. That place was known throughout the city as "Old Withers," and was located on New Levee Street.

"But, if you want something pleasant for the children," he continued, "the house on Royal is far more spacious."

She *did* want something pleasant for the children, and in her unworldliness Margaret thought "reasonable" might perhaps be within her means.

"I'd best be looking at them both," she said. "Will you be coming with me or may I have the keys?"

The man said she could admit herself, and asked to be told of her decision as soon as possible.

She went at once to the "haunted house" on Royal Street. It was situated in the Vieux Carré (Old Square), the core of the fashionable Creole section. Grilled ironwork closed the entrance, but as she glanced up and down the street, it seemed to her unlikely anyone would try to enter—because, as she stood there, most passers-by actually did detour in a wide circle rather than pass the place. Even the bolder ones,

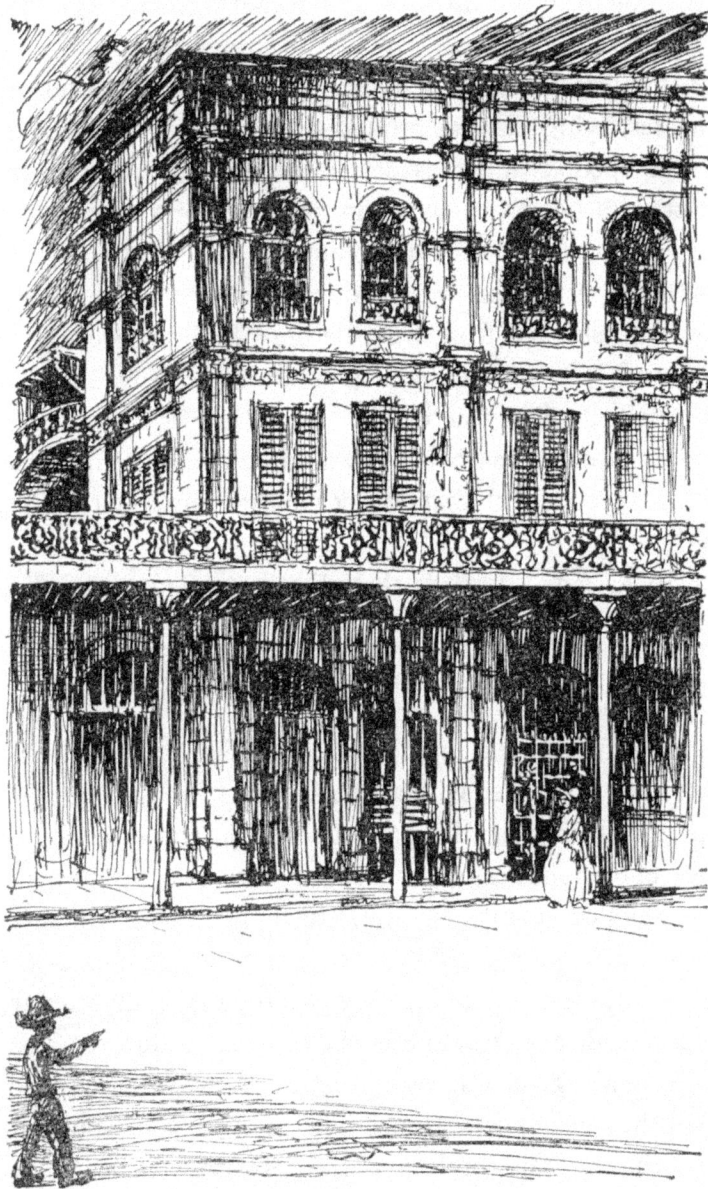

Margaret went to the "haunted house" on Royal Street

unwilling to admit silly superstitions, unconsciously hurried their steps.

After this had happened many times, Margaret wondered what terrifying tales had produced such an effect on sensible-looking people. She was determined to find out, for the practical aspects of having no deliveries or visitors could place the orphanage at a disadvantage.

Her investigation was made simple by a young Negro boy, who shouted from what he must have believed a safe distance: "You'd better get away from there, lady. That's no place to be fooling 'round."

Margaret approached her would-be rescuer, and asked, "What's wrong with that house? I'm thinking about moving in there."

"Lawd, lady—don't do that! That house is haunted, sure enough."

"Bosh!" Margaret replied. "Would you like to go in with me and see?"

Instead of answering, the boy ran down the street, and, in his haste, collided with a woman who had just come from the French market. Her produce fell and scattered all over the cobblestones. Now, thoroughly terrified, the unhappy boy stooped to pick up the strewn fruit and vegetables, while their owner shrilly scolded. After her belongings were retrieved, she marched briskly down the street but, Margaret noted, made a wide detour as she passed 1140 Royal.

Now Margaret was really distressed. If so many people took "haunted houses" this seriously, never a soul would look in at the children's smiling faces. This idea made her hesitate even to examine the interior. She would go for a stroll and think.

Not having often been in the old section of the city,

Margaret moved down Royal Street, marveling at the simplicity of line combined with the delicate cast-iron grillwork of the elegant homes in the French section. She made her way to the Old Square, an area so symmetrical it might have been designed by a child with building blocks. The St. Louis Church—or Cathedral —was flanked by twin buildings, the Cabildo and the rectory; the other facing twins were the Pontalba Buildings, massive structures relieved by lacy cast-iron balconies. Nearby flowed the river, embracing the settlement in a curve, thus giving New Orleans the name of the Crescent City.

And Margaret knew, as she stood there, that this, her chosen city, had become dear to her heart. Yes, in spite of racial frictions, plagues and floods, nowhere did flowers bloom more abundantly nor birds of every hue give out sweeter song. But to stand there musing did not solve her problem. She may as well cross Canal Street into a zone where she could make herself understood.

About to turn, Margaret heard a friendly voice addressing her.

"Good day, Madame."

And, standing close beside her, was one of the Creole ladies from the boat.

"Good day to you," Margaret replied heartily.

Impulsively, the lovely lady extended her two hands, and while shaking Margaret's, the bangles on her bracelets jingled a merry tune.

"And 'ow is your *pauvre* 'usband?"

When Margaret told of Charles's death and that of her infant baby, the woman exclaimed, " 'Ow sad, 'ow terrible!" And she tucked her arm within the crook of Margaret's, adding warmly, "You must come with—we 'ave a talk. We go to a quiet little café where they have delectable chocolate and little cakes, yes?"

Margaret felt she should not take the time, but could not resist the enthusiasm of one trying so hard to be kind.

"Chocolate and little cakes are pretty rich fare for me," she said.

"*Mon Dieu!*" the lady raised her slim gloved hands in a gesture of disapproval. "Don't tell me, please, you are one of those Puritans who believe a little pleasure is sinful."

"I was not thinking about sin," Margaret said, "but my waistline. With the shortness of me, I can't afford extra pounds without looking dumpy." She was forced to add, though, that sometimes the faces of the poor made her feel guilty if she ate too much.

Such an attitude, the woman said, was perfectly acceptable, perfectly. Saints she held in high esteem, but Puritans, ah, *non!*

As they sat sipping their rich, delicious chocolate, Margaret asked about the haunted house on Royal Street. With animation and much gesturing, her newfound friend explained that the fine old home had been inhabited by a beautiful but cruel woman named Madame Lalaurie. Very fashionable, very chic, Madame had entertained lavishly. She was thought to have been a pious woman—charitable and good— until—

She leaned forward now and spoke more softly, in tones holding a hint of the horror to come. It seemed a fire had broken out in the home of Madame Lalaurie and that those who had gone to extinguish the flames uncovered the fact that Madame was absolutely a fiend, absolutely! She had resisted those who had wished to go to the third floor and make sure that everyone was safe. But an adamant gentleman, who had long suspected evil things were going on in the house, insisted that the doors on the top story be unlocked. A group of pitiful mutilated slaves were discovered, having for months been shackled there.

"I did not myself go to the calaboose to see the poor tortured victims," the woman went on, "but thousands of people did. The jailyard was filled with instruments of torture from that house on Royal Street. Why are you especially interested in the place?"

Margaret explained about her visit to the realtor, and said that the gentleman had suggested two houses, both supposedly haunted.

"*Two?*"

"Yes, the other is a house on New Levee Street— Old Withers, he called it. But when I saw how people avoided this first place, I did not even go. Perhaps tomorrow, after I have discussed the problem with Sister Regis, I will return again."

Delicately, the pretty Creole shivered. "Old Withers is 'orrible," she said. "No God-fearing ghost would be caught alive there!" She was silent for a moment, then exclaimed, "Do not look so serious, *cherie.* I do not believe these tales of flashing lights, dragging chains and groans."

"Why is Old Withers so horrible?"

"It is a dirty, old, run-down shack. It could have been a storehouse for the cutthroat pirates, the Lafitte brothers."

"I see," Margaret said. "Then you think the house on Royal Street would be better?"

"That depends. After Madame Lalaurie made her escape, a mob broke into the house—it was rumored the place was completely wrecked. So, *cherie,* all I can advise is that you look for yourself."

Margaret said she probably would.

The Creole lady drew on her soft suede gloves. She must hurry home for a dinner appointment, and later an evening at the opera. Before leaving, however, she gave Margaret her card and promised to interest her friends in the orphanage.

"If they are afraid of haunted houses," she added, "I shall tell them that you—what is your name, *cherie?*"

"Margaret Haughery."

"Hau-ah-ah—"

But she couldn't pronounce the name, so Margaret said what she had to little Paul, "Tell them, just Margaret."

"I will say that you, Margaret, are a match for any ghost," the lady said as they parted. The tall, slim Creole figure moved gracefully down the street, her sheer bouffant skirt swaying from side to side.

It was too late to see Old Withers then. Besides, Margaret was too confused about people's fear of ghosts to make any decision without advice. She crossed Canal Street, to the American section, then hurried to what was "home." Wherever children needed her *was* home, ghosts or no ghosts. What blithering nonsense!

When Margaret recounted her experience to Sister Regis, the nun listened interestedly to every detail. A practical woman, she thought nothing should be decided until Margaret had seen the inside of both houses and found out how much the rents would be. She did not take too seriously Margaret's fears that no one would want to come and see the children. Fears would vanish when it was seen no harm came to those living there.

"At least," Sister Regis said, "*sensible* people will forget this foolishness and come to visit us. So if you are willing again to risk being considered an eccentric, I think it would be wise for you to go inside both houses."

Margaret said she would, the following day.

Sister Regis then asked the name of the Creole lady who had befriended her, and Margaret admitted not even having looked at the card which was stowed away in her handbag. She went to fetch it at once.

"Here it is—let me see—'Madame Jacques Boré,' " Margaret read.

"Boré!" Sister Regis repeated. "The name is an old one in Louisiana. Jean Étienne de Boré was the first mayor of New Orleans. Perhaps your kind friend is a descendant."

"Perhaps," Margaret replied. "Anyhow, she is very gracious, and I enjoyed our little feast."

"That reminds me," Sister Regis said. "You must know, Margaret, that you are not subject to the discipline of our rule. Our routine is very severe, and our fare adequate only for those who have become accustomed to it."

Margaret laughed. "Never fear," she said, "I will not starve. As I told Madame Boré, I am easily inclined to put on weight, which my height does not favor. As for the stern routine— since childhood, I am accustomed to hard work."

"It is up to you, Margaret," Sister Regis told her. "And tomorrow you will again be my emissary?"

"That I will."

It was rather early the following morning when she fitted a key in a lock on the wrought-iron gate at 1140 Royal Street. Despite the hour, the few passers-by stopped in their tracks to watch what must have seemed to them a mad woman crossing the threshold of some sinister unknown.

Margaret was staggered by the lavish ornamentation on the gate, first barrier to entrance. It was magnificently wrought in Empire motif, the vestibule lined with black and white marble, and the massive wooden front door richly carved. Never had she seen such grandeur!

Though Margaret placed small credence in tales of ghostly visitations, she felt a slight twinge of fear as she turned the wrought-iron handle leading into the house. Long unused, the hinges groaned in protest when she shoved in the door. Margaret cast one final glance over her shoulder at the sunlit street. The crowd outside had greatly increased. People probably thought she'd never come out again alive!

Bosh and nonsense! To show her disdain for such folly, she closed the door with a smart little bang and gazed around. Even ruthless destruction could not erase the breathless beauty the house once had. Although huge gaps stood between the mahogany rails of the staircase—where hatchets and clubs had done their work—its graceful sweep upward full three storys was like the liquid curve of a lovely river. As Margaret mounted the stairs, the touch of her hand sent loosened rails downward. They hit the floor below and sounds of their crash were repeated in echoes. Most likely, she thought, the displacement of timber accounted for many of the tales of ghostly presences.

On the second floor she found three large drawing rooms, opening one into the other through sliding doors. Such an arrangement could provide much needed privacy, or, should a larger space be required, the doors could be rolled back. She was now seeing the old house in two ways—the most important as a possible orphanage. But, she could also form a mental picture of the early elegance of this stately mansion.

Everywhere were indeed ghostly remnants of bygone days. In one corner lay a heap of shattered crystal, relic of a chandelier that had hung from large plaster rosettes on the ceilings. A slab of brass encrusted with enamel—once an exquisite tabletop—lay twisted and battered on the floor.

She went on to what had been the sleeping quarters. Here her feet met with curious softness. At first it seemed as if high-piled carpeting had not been removed. Actually, the substance was a mixture of dust and what remained of slashed feather beds.

Mounting the stairs again, she was careful not to brush against the loosened rails. The third story, low-ceilinged, dank and dismal, conveyed the stench of evil. It was here, Margaret remembered, that the tortured victims of Madame Lalaurie had been confined. The thought of their groaning misery actually did conjure up a parade of ghostly visitors.

Hurriedly, she went onto the roof, where from a cupola the view was magnificent. She could see the Mississippi embracing the Old Square, and gazing over the city roofs, Congo Square where the Negroes held their voodoo dances. Below, lay a terraced garden and the slave wing, and above, a vast blue cloudless dome—God's great outdoor cathedral.

After descending the spiral staircase again, she made a practical appraisal of the house and all its possibilities. The place would be ideal! True, it would take a little time to remove the debris, scrub the floors and replace the windowpanes which had all been broken by the angry mob— an action Margaret could but feel justified when she thought of Madame Lalaurie's wanton wickedness. It was not up to her to judge but she could not rid herself of the thought that the fashionable grand lady got what she deserved!

Moving out into the street again, she heard cries of relief from the gathering outside. A few of the more venturesome allowed curiosity to overcome their fears, and moved from what had seemed a safe distance to crowd around Margaret.

What had she seen in there? Had she heard any moans—chains dragging on the stairway?

No, she told her excited questioners, not a single ghost.

This news was relayed to the others who had remained apart. With Gallic realism, they now supposed that if the woman had gone in there and survived, perhaps stories associated with the house were not true.

Margaret did not wait to hear the final opinion, because their animated gestures and earnest speech suggested the crowd might not disperse for hours. And she had another haunted house to visit!

Confronting Old Withers on New Levee Street, in the section of the city known as the Irish Channel, Margaret thought how aptly the house had been christened. Now she well understood why Madame Boré had called it " 'orrible." The wretched old property was brown and wrinkled, and even if it had not been supposedly "haunted," it still would have the air of a deserted outcast. After the beauty of the other house, Margaret did not even want to enter. This was no place for her hapless orphans! Still—she had best go in.

Not only did *these* hinges also groan, but the one on top was broken, so when she pushed the door it slanted at a dangerous angle. The interior did indeed suggest an unsavory storehouse where the Lafitte brothers may have hidden their victims' corpses, along with lawless plunder. Unpartitioned except where spiders had woven their thready screens, there could be no privacy in the vast unbroken area. She eyed a narrow stairway leading up to a loft, but the planks were so mildewed and rotten Margaret was afraid to mount them. From above eerie sounds filtered down—winged insects, the scurry of a rat or a squirrel.

In a surge of wishful thinking that the house on Royal

Street would become their home, Margaret briefly surveyed Old Withers and went outside again.

Then came an unlooked-for complication: she could not close the door. To tug and strain with all her might was of no avail. She didn't know what to do.

Although there was little inside for anyone to take, she had been given the keys and it was her responsibility to make the place secure. Breathless, she heaved again, but the door would not budge.

Then, like a sound from heaven, came a voice close to her side.

"And sure, let me help you."

Above her towered a husky lad, his face Irish as a shamrock.

"I don't believe it will ever close again," Margaret wailed.

"It will," the young man told her assuringly. "Like this, now—we've got to hoist it up a bit."

With ease he raised the heavy wooden panel, then slowly inched it forward. After a final tug, the door settled in its frame, latch clicking.

"It's very grateful to you I am," Margaret said. "You've plenty of strength in those arms."

The young man flushed with pleasure at her praise. " 'Tis nothing after digging ditches, and canals—But might I ask you, ma'am, what is a lady like you doing in Old Withers?"

Margaret told about her search for a proper place to house the orphans. And about Sister Regis who, limited in her work by lay authorities, wanted for her Sisters a foundation of their own. After seeing Old Withers, though, it seemed fit only for the present occupants—vermin, spiders, rats!

Although the young man threw back his head and laughed, he did not quite agree with Margaret. Assuredly, the place was in bad repair and not very cheerful, but much could be done with a little carpentry and paint. He felt sure that for such a worthy cause many volunteers would lend a hand.

He said he had to hurry then, or he'd be late for work. But he'd be keeping his eye on the place, and if the Sisters decided to move in there, he'd round up some helpers from the Channel.

" 'Twould be a good way to get some of the young ruffians off the street," was his parting shot, and before Margaret had the chance to express her thanks, the long, muscled legs of the young man had carried him quite a distance. He turned once, though, and called back to her, "My name's Patrick Murphy."

What good fortune it was that he'd come along, Margaret thought. She felt easier in her mind about Old Withers, but it was the house on Royal Street she was hankering for. Resolutely, she turned her steps in the direction of the realtor.

The Creole gentleman was as courteous as before. Indeed, he beamed at Margaret, bubbling over with good news. The owners of the house on Royal Street had made a most reasonable offer, he said. And, since she had seen both places, there could be no question of a choice.

Margaret's heart pounded with excitement. She could already visualize the babies in one of the drawing rooms, closed off from noise and contagious illness by a handsome sliding door. But the man was speaking—

". . . so they would be willing to lease the place—which is one of the finest on Royal Street—for $200 a month."

Margaret's shocked expression must have conveyed the idea she meant to bargain, and Creoles were good at bargaining.

"Maybe," he said, "$175—"

This was only a little less than Margaret had altogether managed to save.

"I'm sorry," she said weakly, "but we have practically nothing. I—I thought you understood—"

"Just what did you have in mind?" the realtor asked.

"Maybe, $10 a month at the most."

"*Mon Dieu!*" the gentleman exclaimed. "*Dix* dollars."

Miserably, Margaret went on, "I'm sorry to have taken up your time."

When tears of disappointment filled her eyes, the Creole gentleman said soothingly, "No, not at all. You must not despair. After all, Old Withers is available. Even though it is not exactly what we might wish—the cost will be little more than renovation—merely a token payment."

"I suppose it will have to do," Margaret said.

Her disappointment was somewhat eased by the recollection of Patrick Murphy. At least, he had pointed out a way.

"Thank you very much for your trouble," Margaret said.
"Not at all."

Then, instead of shaking her outstretched hand, the dapper gentleman kissed it.

Embarrassed by what she considered a foolish foreign custom, Margaret hastily pulled her arm away. She thought then, that life had taught her well that what couldn't be cured must be endured. And already her practical mind was forwarding the ideas set into motion by her meeting with Patrick Murphy.

Old Withers would have to be scrubbed from top to bottom and painted; and perhaps there would be a way to set up partitions. And when the stairs to the loft were repaired, who knew what possibilities the upper part would hold? Already she could feel a scrubbing brush in her hand, smell fresh paint and hear the reassuring sound of hammer against nail. Besides, Margaret thought, since the place was practically free except for repairs, and these, perhaps, might be made by a core of volunteers, her own funds could provide small luxuries.

When she again faced Sister Regis and told her of the situation, no trace of disappointment was apparent in her voice.

"I have found us a place to live, Sister," she said. "Old Withers on New Levee Street."

The wise woman facing her did not even ask about the other. She simply said, "With God's help, we will manage very well there."

"But much work must be done before we move in," Margaret cautioned. "I will attend to that."

"Thank you, child," Sister Regis replied, then added softly, "Although you have been with us for only a few weeks, Margaret, it seems impossible that we should have gotten on without you."

"Thank you, Sister," Margaret said. "Now, I have little to give except myself, but someday—"

Sister Regis was silent as Margaret dreamed. "Someday, I am going to earn enough money to provide for everyone who needs my help."

When Sister smiled at what must have seemed like youthful boasting, Margaret amended her speech. "Anyhow, that's what I am going to try to do."

"Perhaps you may. But always remember, Margaret, that the 'self' you give, will always be more precious than any worldly goods."

"I will remember, Sister."

Sounds of many feet moving in the corridor told that the children were on their way to supper.

"Paul has been asking for you," Sister Regis said. "You do have a way with children, Margaret."

"That's because I love them. Now, I'd best be getting on and help Sister with supper. First, though, I want to look in at the babies."

The next day, Margaret went to see Father Mullon. She found him at the rectory. A fine friend he was and never too busy to see her, but this time Margaret felt a little ill at ease at not having first consulted him about the children's shelter.

He listened attentively as she told about her visit to the realtor and subsequent experiences with "haunted" houses.

"So Old Withers it will have to be," she said. "And I thought, perhaps, Father, you might help me get in touch with Patrick Murphy, who so generously expressed willingness to help."

"That might be possible," he said. "But if I announce in my pulpit, 'Wanted one Patrick Murphy,' most likely a dozen candidates would appear." He smiled (Father Mullon was a terrible tease), then went on with pretended seriousness, "Anyhow, I'm surprised at you, Margaret Haughery, to even consider that fine house on Royal Street. Is it St. Louis or Joan of Arc you want the innocent children to have as their patron saints? What would our St. Patrick say? Besides, they'd all be going to the Cathedral, where—as one of my loyal parishioners said—'God speaks only in French.' I'm surprised at you, a good Irish woman!"

Though she knew the priest was jesting, Margaret replied quite seriously, "It does, though, trouble me sometimes, Father, all the bad feeling existing between the Creoles and the English-speaking people. Should we not all be united?"

"These things take time, Margaret," Father Mullon said. "Time, or a threat to ideals mutually shared. For instance," he went on, "during the War of 1812." He told her he had often heard his predecessor, Father Kindelon, speak of those frantic days when the British were bent on capturing Louisiana. Aware of the friction between Creoles and Americans, the enemy had printed circulars in French and Spanish. These pamphlets read: "Louisianans! Remain quiet in your houses; your slaves shall be preserved to you, and your property respected. We make war only against Americans."

But this propaganda had not worked. Not only did the Creoles and English-speaking citizens of New Orleans gather on the plains of Chalmet under the leadership of General Jackson, but companies of Kentuckians, Acadians from the streams and bayous of inland Louisiana, flaxen-haired German pioneers who had come to America a hundred years before. Companies of Negroes—"free men of color"—also stood shoulder to shoulder and fought as Americans.

Here Father Mullon smiled, then went on, "Even the brothers Lafitte and their cutthroat bandits were allowed to do battle—probably wearing gold ornaments they'd plundered from their comrades!"

"And they trounced the British, though outnumbered two to one!" Margaret said.

"You've learned your history well, Margaret." Then he looked serious and spoke sadly. "Much of the spirit of 1812 has been forgotten. Too many so-called Americans feel that any kind of foreignness is un-American. And none are less loved than the Irish immigrant. True, sometimes the poor creatures do not behave as well as they should—but then, who does?"

"Who does, indeed?" Margaret observed. "And, if it's first families the Americans are giving themselves airs about, what do the Indians have to say about that?" Both smiled, and after they were silent for a moment, Margaret returned to the subject of Old Withers.

"A terrible shape the place is in," she said. "Do you think people will stay away because it's supposed to be haunted?"

"No," Father said. "And now we must try to round up your handsome Patrick Murphy. But, Margaret, are you sure the life you've chosen is what you really wish? You are a young woman—and very personable. Might you not want children of your own?"

"Who said the lad Murphy was handsome?" she demanded. "None of your matchmaking, Father!"

Then she gazed down at her hands folded in her lap, and went on softly, "Charles was my love. I don't think I'll ever be wanting another. This is the work I want to do."

"You will do it well, Margaret, and others be rewarded for the doing. And, please know, my good friend, you can always count on me for help."

4

THE HAPPY BEGGAR

In Margaret's mind, Old Withers was already spruced up, painted and topped with a new roof. This fantasy made the place even more unattractive as she approached it for the second time. Brown and rutted, the old shack suggested to her enormous prunes piled one upon the other. Rain had fallen through the night, and New Levee Street—normally unpaved and rutted—was now a network of runlets.

A short distance away, where rain had cut deep in the center of the street, a bespattered goat floundered in the water, trying to gain a foothold on the slippery mud. Shrill cries came from an alleyway between two unpainted hovels, and a little girl appeared. Though she screamed and scolded, "Come back here you—you—" her bare feet slithered happily through the muddy water until she reached the goat.

As she hauled at some kind of a collar around the creature's neck, her words became those of an adult who, though disgusted, still spoke with tolerant affection. "You stupid, foul-smelling, lazy drunk. If I catch you behaving like this again, I'll bash your head in." This was said in exact imitation of many of the wives in the Irish Channel, when meager house money had been frittered away in some saloon.

After a mighty tug, the goat got a grip on a patch of sodden earth, and seeming to understand the dire threats, trotted obediently toward the child. She, on the other hand, was not yet ready to abandon the pleasant feel of water trickling between her toes. She kicked, sending a spray in Margaret's direction.

Startled, fearful almost, the little girl gazed at the stranger about to enter Old Withers. "You goin' in there?" she asked.

"Yes," Margaret said.

"It's haunted, that house," the child said.

"Oh, I don't believe that. I'm not afraid."

"Me neither."

Margaret thought that perhaps here in the Irish Channel where sickness, poverty, and violence were commonly accepted, real misery held more terror than fables about ghosts. She wondered then if the Irish Channel, with its poorly lighted muddy streets and the stench from the slaughterhouse on the riverbank, might not welcome the orphans of the poor with more understanding than in a better neighborhood.

"I'm glad you're not afraid," Margaret told the little girl, "because this house will be filled with boys and girls—even babies."

As if not to be outdone, the child boasted, "We have three babies in our house. The twins, Bridget—then I come. And my big brothers and sisters—and, oh, yes, Jude—that's the goat. Sometimes, she's a blithering nuisance."

"Jude . . . she?"

"Sure. Tim—that's my oldest brother—says it doesn't matter. St. Jude does the impossible. So—well, our goat gives us milk. If she didn't, we wouldn't have any—see?"

"I see," Margaret said. "But now I'd better be getting inside, and I hope you'll come to see the children when we move in."

"Can't I go in now?"

The child followed Margaret up to the door, which, after being unlocked, refused to budge.

"Sure, Patrick Murphy slammed it in place for keeps," Margaret said.

"He'll be along in a little while," the child announced. "Maybe he can climb in one of the windows."

"You know Patrick Murphy, then?"

"Sure, everyone knows Pat. Here he comes now!"

So he was, striding down the street, a fine figure of a lad. It suddenly came to Margaret that Patrick was no more of a lad than she was a lass; suffering had made her feel old beyond her years. Father Mullon's teasing came back to her, and suddenly she wanted to run away. She could climb in a window herself—didn't need help from anyone.

It was too late, though, because young Murphy had breached the gap between them. His eyes were clear and honest, his smile impersonal. There was no need for her to run.

"I see you're having trouble with the door again," he said, then, ruffling the child's unkempt hair, added, "And how is Annie O'Toole this day?"

"Fine. Jude ran away and got stuck in the mud. Now, I want to go inside with this lady."

Pat turned to Margaret and asked, "When are you thinking of moving in?"

"As soon as possible," she told him.

"Supposing this might be so," Patrick Murphy said, "I've already spoken to some of my friends who are handy with hammer and saw. So, if you give me leave, within a week or two we'll get the place in fit condition."

When she started to protest, Patrick explained that until the roof was patched, stairs to the loft repaired, and the place ridden of vermin and rodents, scrubbing brushes and dust cloths would be useless.

Margaret had to admit this was so.

"And I'm deeply grateful to you for all your trouble," she told him. "I would be at a loss to look for laborers. We do have money to pay for the services." Patrick said this was a matter they could discuss later. No, Margaret told him, they'd have to discuss it now. She went on about the workmen being worthy of their hire, and why should they who were giving up their time not expect to receive a wage?

"What about the Sisters?" Patrick asked, "and you —I can imagine you're receiving a very handsome salary?"

"That's different."

"Why?"

"What I am doing is what I've chosen to do."

"Well, then," Patrick said a trifle angrily, "be generous enough to let others decide what *they* want to do. If there are those who wish to be paid, I'll let you know."

His words struck a special chord in Margaret. Maybe, in pride, she did not give credit to others for their willingness to share!

She looked into the clear blue eyes of Patrick Murphy and said, "Thank you for reminding me of a shortcoming. We'll be grateful for any help."

Patrick tried the door again, which stuck at first. But when he used his whole weight, it swung in, tilted, then came the slam of wood against wood after the rusty hinge gave way.

This surprising crash was too much for Annie O'Toole who, after a brief glimpse of the gloomy interior, turned and ran down the street.

Inside the dreary house, Margaret asked Pat what he thought of certain possibilities—perhaps a partition here, a partition there. Some shelves near the rickety stove for a few dishes—and maybe the loft could also be divided to provide an area of privacy.

He listened and made notes, assuring her that he would come as close to her suggestions as possible.

"And when the place is secure from the elements," he said, "I will send word to the Poyders Asylum. Your name—?"

"Just say Margaret."

A child cried out in the night. This sound was soon echoed by other voices and small heads were raised from pallets on the floor. Then came the soothing voice of a young novice, the hiss of a match before the candle burst into a flame. But the pale circle of light did not at once dispel all fear. The place was strange, and, in the memories of orphans, altered situations had meant illness, death, and parting. Thus change was suspect, a condition to be feared.

"I'm lost," came a shrill, plaintive wail.

Then, Sister saying softly, "No! you must all be quiet now. This is our new home."

But giving the scene a name only partially removed doubts of the unknown. It was Paul, with his cowlick and mischievous face, who shamed some into silence by saying, "Girls! Can't you stop your sniveling and let us go to sleep."

Almost-quiet descended then, and Sister blew out her

candle. Not total quiet, though, for there still remained a soft trail of muffled sobs.

Sure-footed even in the dark, Margaret moved down between the pallets. She had arranged them and knew precisely where loneliness concealed its anguish on a hard straw pallet.

"I'm lost," the child had wailed.

And Margaret was again a little girl, with parents suddenly removed, so long ago. Her hand sought the shaking little figure and she whispered, "It's Margaret." She felt small, slender arms reach up and cling as her own clasped the shivering body close and she rocked and whispered, "There, there—"

Tighter the arms clung, and a hot, wet cheek pressed against her own, shifted and moved until the child's lips breathed in her ear, "I'm frightened, Margaret." Softly she answered, "And sure, we're all frightened sometimes, pet."

"All—?"

"All."

She rocked again and again, until gradually the jerking sobs subsided, the arms relaxed and—not quite yet—but soon, a sigh, content and unafraid and small arms let go their hold.

Gently, Margaret lowered the little girl to her pallet, and quietly sought her own.

But she could not sleep. Although the odor of fresh paint reminded her that Patrick Murphy and his crew had refused to be paid for their labor, in spite of donations from a few rich parishioners outside the Channel, the future seemed bleak and hazardous. Then, remembering that Sister Regis never batted an eye when she first saw the Withers (indeed she had behaved as if the place was quite a find), Margaret was ashamed of her timidity. Still—all of their futures depended on charity, and those in the Channel had so little to spare. Her thoughts were briefly set aside by whimpering of an infant. What if this were her own little Frances! Suddenly, then, resoluteness overcame her doubts. Yes, they were all beggars. But she, Margaret Haughery, who would be loathe to ask a crumb for herself, was about to become the best beggar in all New Orleans! Calmness descended and she fell asleep.

Weeks passed and the children grew accustomed to their home. Patrick Murphy came one day to hack down weeds in a small place at the rear now called the "garden." Tangle-haired Annie from down the street was a frequent visitor. Sometimes she dragged the reluctant Jude around to the rear for the dual purpose of feeding the goat and keeping the grass short-cropped. Some of the neighbors called, and some more fearful stayed away.

The women who wanted to help, Margaret occasionally pressed into service, to sew, patch here and there, fit hand-me-downs; but when fabric gave out they must wait because Sister Regis insisted that Margaret should not touch her own funds, except for a trifle here and there. All else must be saved for a possible emergency. "Emergency" meant unlimited threats: the day when there would not be even enough for food, the month when the plague might strike and medicines be needed, the year—

"Year!" Margaret would retort. "Why, by then everyone will know our needs and be flooding us with bounty."

"Oh, Margaret—" Sister's words sounded a reminder of reality.

Actually Margaret *knew*, because she had discovered that

even the best of beggars, such as she, usually returned with paltry gifts. Yet she was learning more and better techniques for approaching even the most hardhearted. She always assumed that a prospective donor was eager to give—and even the smallest token merited high praise from her.

She became a well-known figure on the Channel streets, hauling along a broken-down cart, hammered together by one of Patrick's workmen. It had become the habit of a young Negro lad to trail along with her. He was a rickety, undernourished boy, whose hollow cheeks and sorrowful expression defied all speculation about his age. His look of having been totally abandoned touched Margaret's motherly heart.

At first, she supposed that he went along merely out of curiosity. Later, discovering that the wretched child used any opportunity to pilfer a morsel of food from her cart, she arranged for him to be her helper—carrying bundles into the house or, when the mood struck him, of pretending he was a donkey pulling the cart along. For these labors, he was given a share of the food, and out of money donations a small amount was set aside for him.

His only concrete information was that his name was "Jackson." To Margaret's query, "After the General?" the boy replied he didn't know. Nor could he say whether it was his first or last name, but it was the only one he had.

"Well," Margaret told him, "you are just 'Jackson' and I am just 'Margaret,' so we should get along very well."

Still, some remnant of an early attitude dictated that he should call her "*Miss* Margaret."

Typical of Margaret's experiences was the day she visited a grocer who seemed more prosperous than many in the Channel. Though previous encounters had taught her that

Jackson pretended to be a donkey, pulling the cart along

those faring better were less likely to be generous, she stepped across the threshold hopeful and smiling broadly.

She was greeted with high-voiced intonation, "I know ye, Margaret, and there's no use of your stepping in."

"I am in."

Cheerfully she gazed at the sallow little man whose pennies she felt sure were as pinched as his cheeks.

"I told ye—"

"Now, all I'm stopping for—and I can tell by the kindness on your face you wouldn't begrudge me—is a drink of water in this weather."

His face did become kinder, and he said, of course, she was more than welcome to a glass of water. As she slowly sipped, Margaret intermingled glances with a barrage of Blarney.

"And I've always been saying about you, Mr. O'Shay, there's no man in the neighborhood more deserving of success. Prudence is a quality not given to all, I tell them. 'Waste not, want not' is the kind of man you are, Mr. O'Shay."

She set the glass down on the counter.

What was almost recognizable as a faint smile came to his lips. "I hadn't been told you were such a wise woman," said Mr. O'Shay.

"That I am not," Margaret replied modestly. "Wisdom is for men like yourself, Mr. O'Shay, who, I'm sure wouldn't want to throw out those empty potato bags when they could be put to good use."

"Good use—empty potato bags?"

"Yes, nothing better for making boys suits—especially fine for the winter."

Mr. O'Shay agreed this was a frugal and splendid idea, and Margaret left with four bags, one reassuringly heavy enough to foretell potato soup for dinner!

Time passed, then one day in autumn, a season so little differing from all the others since the change between all seasons was slight, something unusual happened at Old Withers. Margaret, who was in the garden with a group of younger children, received a hurried summons to go indoors. It seemed she had a visitor, and not one from the neighborhood.

Hurrying to the fore of the building, she found Sister Regis engaged in an animated conversation with Madame Jacques Boré. Nearby stood a smiling liveried Negro. After warmly clasping Margaret's hands, the lovely Creole explained that her servant had left her coach a few blocks away; she would not have dared bring it into that " 'orrible" neighborhood. As it was, her faithful Thomas had been insulted, jeered at because of his livery, and all in all, their brief walk had been devastating.

After a cool drink, however, which was brought by a young Sister, Madame Boré again took up the talk with Sister Regis, telling that her daughter Cécile, who like most of the young ladies of New Orleans studied at the Ursuline Academy, had outgrown a great many of her clothes. And, since the house on Royal Street was still vacant, she'd imagined—as Margaret predicted—that they'd moved into this dreary, hideous place. So she'd decided to come with the outgrown garments and a few gifts for *"les pauvres enfants."* Never again, though, would she step into this neighborhood—*jamais!*

Although Madame Boré rattled on about the inconvenience caused her and cast shocked glances at the orphans "costumes," it was obvious she was kind and warm, merely covering her profound pity for their poverty.

"So," she ended, "you, Margaret, will hereafter have to call on me. Anyhow," —she raised her gloved hand in protest— "you can't get blood from an onion. So, if you must be a beggar, find someone to haul your cart to the French Quarter. You might even get donations from the *nouveaux riches* Americans in the Garden District. I doubt it, though. One cannot be that rich and also generous, no?"

Though Sister Regis obviously reserved judgment, her smile conveyed complete understanding.

Then Madame Boré asked where Thomas should put the boxes she brought. "Your children will have a feast tonight," she said. "This is the anniversary of my first meeting with dear Margaret. Everyone will have little cakes and chocolate."

Margaret's joyful cry, making it seem there was nothing in the world so needed by the children, was not exactly hypocritical. It was so rare the orphans had a feast—and never before had it been cakes and chocolate! She was determined to make it a really special occasion.

Sister Regis left the room with Thomas to put the perishables in the large, outmoded ice chest and the boxes of clothing behind a partition they called the storeroom. And after a while Margaret also excused herself to seek Sister out and tell her she would like to walk with Madame Boré and Thomas to their carriage. If Margaret accompanied her, the strangers would be identified as guests of the orphanage and spared further jeers and insults.

"By all means go, Margaret," Sister Regis said.

"I will. And on the way back, I mean to stop and buy some milk." When Sister Regis seemed about to protest, she went on hurriedly, "Sure, this *is* an emergency. Let's not spoil that glorious chocolate by diluting it with water."

"Very well, Margaret. Tonight we will not economize."

After that unforgettable meal and when the children were in bed, Sister Regis and Margaret unpacked the clothes brought by Madame Boré. Besides those outgrown by her daughter—sheer cottons with hand-stitched tucks—Madame Boré had included a few of her own costumes. Cécile's sheer frocks could be cut down to make dresses for the babies, but Madame Boré's finery—Well, the wide, sweeping skirts of a velvet and brocade gown could, if taken apart and neatly stitched together, make pretty quilts to be used on the pallets of the sick when the weather grew cold.

"One need not crave expensive things to recognize their beauty," Sister Regis said, stroking a flower on the green brocade evening gown.

Margaret agreed and the two friends looked at one another. Margaret was certain they shared the very same thought.

"How little do the rich know of the poor!" she burst out.

But Sister's smile was warm and gentle when she said, "Madame Boré is a kind and gracious woman."

"She is, indeed," was Margaret's answer.

5
TREES, COWS AND THE CITY

"What are we going to do?" Sister Regis exclaimed.
Sympathetic as she was with Sister's concern,
Margaret laughed. "Wouldn't you know," she said, "that
after we'd ridden Old Withers of vermin and ghosts it would
suddenly become a valuable property!"

The nun gazed at her reproachfully, waving a sheet of
paper in her hand.

"It isn't like you, Margaret, to assume tones of levity about
a serious matter," she said. "It says here—here —" She shook
the letter again. "The owner is putting the place up for sale
and we'll have to move."

"So be it," Margaret replied, "and good riddance, if you
ask me. This was never a fit place to bring up children. More
than once I've been forced to agree with Madame Boré. Old
Withers *is* 'orrible."

Her exact imitation of Madame Boré's inflection brought a
brief smile to Sister Regis' lips. Then she looked anxious again.

"But what are we going to do, Margaret?"

"Find another place, this time in the country. We'll have sunshine and trees and flowers and cows—"

Close as she could get to exasperation, Sister Regis said, "Stop dreaming, Margaret. Remember, it wasn't easy before for us to find shelter."

"I know, Sister, but it's different now."

"How different?"

Smugly Margaret said, "With my experience of these past few years, I could melt a heart of stone. And, mind you, I'd not even be above a little trickery."

"Why, Margaret—!"

"Don't you be worrying now. I promise not to land in the calaboose."

"I should certainly hope not," Sister Regis said weakly.

But Margaret knew that Sister's concern was halfpretense. The good woman had become accustomed to her impulsive flights, which were more apt to be words than acts of rashness.

Earlier in her wanderings, Margaret had discovered a run-down plantation on the outskirts of the city. Obviously because of its unkempt appearance, the place was vacant. This time she would go directly to the owner and make her appeal in behalf of her innocent charges.

After an appointment had been set up, Margaret's mind started to spin the web of her innocent "trickery." Came the day to inspect the old plantation.

"We'll be taking Paul and Penny along," Margaret told Sister Regis.

Penny, the little girl "lost in the night," had been abandoned on the steps of Poyders Asylum. Margaret often thought that her nickname, "Penny," might have been more aptly "Ha'penny," so slight and fragile was this lovely child.

"If you think so, Margaret," Sister Regis agreed.

Then she turned to one of the older girls, asking that she supervise the children's dressing so they'd look neat and presentable.

Neat, yes, Margaret agreed, but not too presentable. "I think Paul should wear a suit made out of Mr. O'Shay's elegant potato sacks," she said. "As for Penny, the poor child looks forlorn no matter what she has on, so it doesn't matter."

"You wouldn't let the children go dressed like that!" Sister Regis said.

"Wouldn't I, though. Now, don't be looking at me that way, Sister, all's fair in love and war, and this is both!" Then to avoid her friend's vaguely reproachful gaze, Margaret turned away and added, "I'd better wash up a bit myself."

When Margaret appeared in an old calico dress she had brought from Baltimore, patched in many places and usually worn for scrubbing, Sister Regis first shook her head, then burst into gales of hearty laughter.

"Margaret, Margaret! I guess it's my turn to rend my habit."

"No," Margaret said, an arm around each of the forlorn-looking waifs as Paul and Penny came to join them. "I think the three of us will paint a sorry enough picture."

From a livery nearby, they leased a rickety carriage, a lame horse and Sister Regis, Margaret and the two children drove to the plantation. There they met the owner of the house, a mild, aging man, who peered at them uncertainly through pale-blue, watery eyes.

Margaret explained why they had come, and painted a glowing picture of what they had done to renovate their present property and vastly increase its value. The man began to feel that, under such circumstances, it might be an advantage for him to let them have the place. He lived with his son and it was a chore to make frequent trips to the plantation to discourage vandals from destroying his property. His only hesitation was that so many children—who were unaccustomed to the niceties of life—might not appreciate the beauty of his fine old home.

Heavenly saints! Margaret thought. She looked at Paul and Penny. And, what about herself? She could feel the patches on her dress enlarging, deepening in hue, until it seemed she was wearing a patchwork quilt. Serves you right, Margaret Haughery, for your deception! The man was peering through half-closed eyes at the children. Breathlessly, she evoked St. Bridget. She, a brave widow, would be the kind of saint to understand and intercede in such a situation.

"They seem very well behaved," the gentleman said, "but—"

"St. Bridget, St. Bridget, St. Bridget!" Margaret breathed.

"But," he went on, "are the others as mild-mannered and nicely dressed as these?"

There was no irony in his voice, and Margaret felt vague panic for the swift concrete answer that St. Bridget had made to her appeal. She hadn't deserved it!

"Oh, yes, the children usually look much nicer than this." Now, no more deceptions, Margaret, she told herself, and added, truthfully, "Of course, they like to play, romp, it wouldn't be natural if they didn't."

"That's true," the man agreed. Then he went on apologetically, "I do hope you ladies will pardon me if I seem to peer. I broke my spectacles this morning."

Margaret did not have to turn to know that Sister Regis' shoulders were shaking with silent laughter.

While the old gentleman was making up his mind, he took them through a tour of the house, then out to the rear where, although overgrown with weeds, patches of color rose from the tangle of gay flowers that pushed through the fertile Louisiana soil.

When they were shown an old shed and a barn, Margaret broke forth in phrases of high exuberance, "We can fix the shed up for Jackson," she said. "He will be able to help us with the cows."

"Cows," the old man said. "Do you expect to keep cows?"

Her voice tilted in warning, Sister Regis put in, "Margaret—!"

But Margaret was not to be daunted. "Yes," she replied, "we are going to have cows. I will use my own funds, and borrow if need be. It has been my dream for the children to have milk, heavy rich milk and not watered down." Here, she seemed to be thinking aloud, "—And butter and cheese. Yes, I do mean to have cows."

So definite was she that Sister Regis did not argue the matter.

"I like your spirit," the gentleman said. "And I will let you have the place rent free with the understanding that certain repairs will be made, and that I can expect the children not to deface my property."

Promises were solemnly given, and a small, informal paper signed.

Farewell, Old Withers, out into the sunshine. Cows!

Life was infinitely more pleasant at the old plantation. The children could rest in the sun, and now that there were no hazards of the streets, the older girls were allowed to supervise a group of little ones. The nuns thus had more time for teaching.

When news of their departure had been heralded in the

Channel, many people, previously flinching at Margaret's approach, had behaved as if her departure were the occasion for a wake. Mr. O'Shay had appeared at the orphanage with four more potato sacks, and, showing to what heights his generosity ascended, he also brought a box of hardtack. Those unseasoned biscuits, he said, would be good for the children's teeth, and discourage hankering for that which they could not afford.

Most of the other donors were more gracious, especially Patrick Murphy and some of his longshoremen friends, who provided gifts and promised services.

Margaret suspected it was this group of men—whose rough tactics in a fight made them feared throughout the city—who had arranged for transportation to the new home.

Patrick had expressed deep sadness at Margaret's going and promised that he and his friends would drive out to the plantation from time to time. Touched by his consistent helpfulness and generosity, Margaret had thanked him with unusual warmth.

"Sure, I'm going to be lonesome without you," Patrick had said in low, despairing tones.

Because of Father Mullon's teasing and also since she felt Patrick might be building up a romantic attachment, Margaret replied gaily, "Go on with you, now. It's not around the world we're moving. You will be visiting us, and I expect to come back and dance at your wedding."

Margaret remembered the reproachful look he'd given her, but thought Pat would soon find himself a girl in the Channel, one who'd be loving him wholly.

Now, however, she did not have too much time to think about the problem of young Murphy. She was far too busy with the children and her two cows. Thoroughly convinced that the creatures would in the end pay off, she'd been dismayed to discover that her own funds were sufficient to buy only what amounted to a cow and a half! This problem she took to Father Mullon.

"I fear half a cow, Father, wouldn't produce very rich milk. So, would you please try to find someone willing to lend me enough for the other half? Sure, the novelty of this idea should appeal to one of your wealthy parishioners."

They both laughed, then Margaret added seriously that she felt in her bones that given a chance, she might be able to develop a dairy business. Father Mullon did secure her a loan, which was soon paid off.

At first, her wares were in demand mostly by neighbors. Later Margaret extended the area of her business to include the city. Her role as milkmaid is one of those best remembered in New Orleans—an attractive young woman, clear-complexioned, blue-eyed and with a very determined set of chin, driving her cart through the city streets with tall cans of milk at her side.

People felt it was an advantage to have dairy products delivered, especially since the quality of Margaret's was superb. But more than convenience and the superiority of her products, Margaret's warm personality went out to others in a way that made people want her for a friend. Thus she made many friends.

Although the sad faces of the poor had priority in Margaret's heart, she learned that even those that had never known want, those whose lives seemed vain and frivolous, were also lonesome and needed a friend. And since that which she wished for herself was merely a by-product of yearning to give to others, Margaret could be trusted.

She was willing to take chances, to make herself heard and

to ask favors without pride. Thus, on her bumpy journeys over the cobblestoned streets of the city, she made known to all who would listen the plight of the orphans and the poor. The poor, too, made their plight known to her. And never, never could she refuse a sincere plea. Indeed, she felt impelled to give even to shifty-eyed, wheedling characters, whose manner suggested they might be frauds. Maybe they were but, on the other hand, they might be hungry, and this she could not bear.

Margaret usually started on her route early in the morning, first serving her own neighbors before going into the center of the city. It was then that New Orleans was like a lovely lady, aroused from slumber and with a transparent veil drawn about her. Even when the heat became intense, the sun never quite succeeded in dispelling this misty mantle.

Since New Orleans actually lay below sea level, between the Mississippi River and Lake Pontchartrain, the atmosphere was laden with humidity. No matter how neat and starched was Margaret's calico dress when she started out in the morning, by night it was as limp as if it never had been pressed. This same dampness caused the plaster to peel off houses in a matter of months, and toned down the deepest colors into soft pastels.

Those were the first gaudy, lush days of her beloved New Orleans, when money flowed free as the river. When in excess, rising, like the river above the levee, money spilled over and spent itself upon gambling and drunkenness. And Margaret often thought, with all of this abundance, how little was given to the poor!

Still her's was a good lot, and thankful she was to be riding in her rickety old cart, where, with a slight turn of her head, she could see the beauty of God's creation. More glorious than all jewels were the multicolored flowers—jasmine, camellias, magnolias, irises, lilies, poinsettias, and wisteria, weeping huge clusters of purple tears—for their scent brought fragrance and sound: the hum of bees a soft accompaniment to bird song.

Other sounds, too, became part of a rhythmic pattern. Chains clanging, as sweating prisoners mended a canal; the humorous and pathetic nonsense lyrics of Negroes from the West Indies; plantation songs; crude rhymes composed by peddlers sauntering along the streets crying their wares to anyone who would listen. The blackberry woman, who, after a long trek in the woods and bayou banks, roamed the streets, her bare legs protruding from skirts which had been tucked in gypsy fashion around her waist, called in melancholy tones:

"Black-ber-ries—fresh and fine—I got blackberries, lady

Fresh from de vine, I got blackberries, ladies, three glass fro'
a dime,

I got blackberries, I got blackberries, black-berries."

But the most diverse of all noise could be heard in the French Market, where hawkers and patrons vied with one another in bargaining. Madame Boré had told Margaret to go there, especially in the evening when she was homeward bound. If one kept a stiff upper lip and defiantly lowered prices, it was possible to purchase leftovers for practically nothing. Margaret did very well in the French Market, and as she became better known, foodstuffs were handed to her as gifts for *"les pauvre enfants."*

Occasionally, when there was a little time left over, Margaret went to a section of the market where gaily plumed birds chatted in various tongues. By their speech and intonation, previous owners could be classified. Some squawked in polite, low-toned French, while others evoked by their hearty oaths some seaman giving vent to his disdain for effete landlubbers. It fascinated Margaret that even birds could be taught the language of love or hate and reveal the relationships that existed in their previous surroundings.

One evening, as she stood watching the birds, an artist hovered around the cages with his sketch pad. With a kind of magic, he swiftly caught the lines and curves of those lovely feathered creatures. The man seemed to notice no one in the place, only the birds with their multicolored wings which could not beat their way through the wires that imprisoned them.

As he paused for a moment in his sketching, the stranger spied Margaret and gave a slight start of surprise. Then, without apology or fanfare, he spoke to her, saying, "My name is James Audubon. I'm up from the Barataria section where I spend most of my time. Since I am a naturalist, birds and reptiles mean more to me than people, especially the wastrels one finds around New Orleans."

True, the man went on, since one had to eat to live, he was forced to mingle with the wealthy in order to paint their portraits. For the most part, though, their soft, decadent faces filled him with despair.

"But, you now, madame, strike a chord of purposefulness," he said. "Might I be bold enough to inquire what gives you this sense of stability in a rotting atmosphere?"

Margaret threw her head back and laughed. She believed that the stranger only half-meant what he said, and, indeed, her merriment did bring a smile to his lips. She told him about the orphans and her dairy, adding that though in her

The artist hovered around the cages with his sketch pad

wanderings she found some greed and selfishness, if properly approached most people could be moved to kindness.

"Extraordinary," the artist said.

Margaret noticed that as they were talking, he still sketched. Curious, she wanted to see what he was portraying, but thought the question might be disturbing to his work.

"There, I've done it," he said suddenly, and tore a piece of paper from his pad.

"This is for you," he announced, handing her the sheet.

To her utter amazement, Margaret saw her own likeness gazing back at herself, merry-eyed, smiling, and an exact reproduction of her flowered calico dress.

"Why, that's—that's—" Words failed her.

The man said, "Hand it back to me, I'll sign it," and with a flourish, he scrawled his name. "Perhaps someday if the orphans are hungry you might want to try to sell it," he added. "Time will reveal whether my work is of any value."

"Sell it, never!" Margaret said.

"I believe you," the artist told her. "Your sincerity is real, rare and extremely welcome."

He turned back to the birds again.

Though Margaret did not know what a priceless possession she held in her hand, she would again and again hear the name of James Audubon.

6

MARGARET GOES TO A PARTY

As Margaret's dairy business continued to expand, she often recalled her dream of someday having enough to give to everyone who needed her help. Still far removed from this ambitious goal, she had managed nevertheless to save some money. Soon, maybe, the orphans could have a home of their own! Dependent on landlords and their whims, there was always the continued possibility of their being evicted.

Margaret was now less fearful in making plans because she had become gradually convinced that she, who had no need or desire for money herself, nonetheless might become a good businesswoman. She sometimes consulted with Charles Macready and Nicholas Bourke, two men in the parish, whose shrewd judgment had brought them fortunes. After a financial recession in 1837, they, like everybody else, predicted that New Orleans was about to enter a period of great prosperity.

When plans were started to enlarge St. Patrick's Church, which could no longer contain the overflow of people crowding into New Orleans, at once the cry went up that the Cathedral, too, must be enlarged and no less elegant than the church of *les Américains*. To counter the sting that the Creoles had up until then far surpassed Americans in cultural pursuits, an English actor, named James H. Caldwell, built two new theaters, one, the St. Charles, the most magnificent in America. The same James Caldwell, with other civic-minded men, bought farmlands and developed rural homes until wide-open spaces took on the look of suburbia.

Not only did the Americans come, but a tremendous flow of immigrants from across the seas, seeking a haven of freedom. In New Orleans this tide of strangers seemed a threat, because if cheap labor could be had readily, the slave system would be in jeopardy. Fearing their power might be lessened, James Caldwell and his followers formed an organization called the Louisiana Native American Association, and put out a newspaper called *The True American*. This bigoted sheet contained ideas so alien to those of the founding fathers that its name was both ludicrous and false. The editor, John Gibson, took a stand against all foreign-born, as if all Americans except the Indians were not precisely that! It warned that those of despotic tradition and decadent civilizations would never rid themselves of Old World concepts.

The Native Americans used their paper to agitate for laws prohibiting all foreign-born—whether they be naturalized or not—from voting until they had served a twenty-one-year probation in the states. The editor, who had previously championed the Anglo-Americans against the French of Louisiana, now tried to induce those earliest settlers to join in a program for keeping down "the foreigners." Gibson stated that, of course, the French, whose ranks could be counted among the most cultured in America, were not identified with the lowly scum of Irish, Germans, Slavs and French now arriving at the levees in New Orleans.

Politely the Creoles listened and declined to become a party to race-baiting. For, after all, who were Gibson and Caldwell if not foreigners? Who were they now building their spacious homes and enlarging the city boundaries so that the Vieux Carré was almost swallowed up in the midst of sprawling houses? True, the Americans were gaining the ascendancy, but the Creoles had no wish to assist in their upward flight.

Since she was listening to learn, Margaret could not fail to be affected by these many attitudes, nor could she always refrain from taking sides. Why here in this great country, should the *Anglo*-Americans consider themselves above the others? If their families came over on *The Mayflower,* was that not proof they too were trying to get away from tyranny?

She would have liked to discuss these matters with Father Mullon, but he was now taxed to the utmost, combating and denouncing the un-American wave of Nativism now sweeping the city. He felt that, if unchecked, it could result in hostility between Protestant and Catholic.

Although these weighty matters often came into Margaret's mind, the core of her life was supervising her dairy which had expanded greatly. It now required many helpers, including young Jackson, who had become very skillful at his chores and now counted himself the property of "Miss Margaret," along with her other workers. Though she disliked the system of slavery, Margaret considered those who by their toil helped to promote the welfare of her orphans also as her children. That they and their families be well taken care of, she considered a deep and challenging responsibility.

Sometimes Margaret drove to the Channel to visit her old friends. Fresh paint and the fact it was being kept in the pink of condition had not rid Old Withers of its sinister reputation. Tangle-haired Annie O'Toole's family had increased by one baby and two goats. News of Patrick Murphy had him courting a fair colleen, recently arrived from Ireland. And as for Mr. O'Shay, so thriving was his business that he'd been forced to buy an extra building. Indeed the Channel was bursting at its seams, with small, low-rental homes pushing back from the river front, threatening to spill over into other sections.

Sometimes Margaret visited Minna Weber at the St. Charles Hotel; she had been promoted from chambermaid to head of the linen room. On these occasions, Margaret would gaze from the rear window of the hotel and recall that it was from here her new life of happiness had started.

"Ach, and I advised you not to go," Minna would say. "You know what you want to do, Margaret, and you do well." After such words of praise, Minna usually added, "But *why*, my friend, do you always wear such drab dresses like a *madschen* in uniform? You are young, attractive—"

Usually Margaret broke in, denying a need for anything more elaborate than her neat, starched calicos. One time, however, on an afternoon late in the year 1839, she was more agreeable.

"Maybe I should have one dress with a few tucks and flounces," she admitted. "It's been on my mind since I accepted a dinner engagement at Madame Boré's."

"I should think so!" Minna returned.

And before Margaret had a chance to change her mind, Minna burst forth in a torrent of Germanic thrift and efficiency. Margaret was at once to purchase a sheer, flower-patterned cotton. She, Minna Weber, who had always made her daughter's dresses, would fit it and put it together in a few days. Margaret would also need a petticoat with enough body to make the skirt of the dress flare out. The bodice would be softly draped with a ruffle at the neckline—

"Not low," Margaret put in.

"Not low."

True to her word, Minna had the dress finished a week before Madame Boré's small informal dinner party. After Margaret had dressed, she exhibited her new gown for Sister Regis' approval.

"You look charming, Margaret," Sister said. "But haven't you any beads or ornaments to give a little color to your costume?"

Margaret did have one brooch of beaten gold, inherited from her mother. In its center was the worn enameled coat of arms of the O'Rourkes. This, along with a few other family pieces, had been carefully stowed away by Mrs. Richards until her adopted daughter had been old enough to care for them. Because of the painful associations of her parents' death, Margaret had never worn the brooch. Now, though, she mentioned it to Sister.

"Wear it by all means, Margaret. To exhibit a prized heirloom is not vanity. Indeed, it's another kind of pride to deny one's honorable ancestry."

Only the family and a few close friends were at the dinner party. Madame Boré explained that she'd long wanted her husband, Jacques, to meet Margaret, and also her daughter

Cécile, whose frivolous attitude sometimes caused her parents despair. Though Monsieur Boré nodded in agreement, both parents beamed lovingly at their beautiful young daughter who seemed not to be taking their criticism too seriously. She looked up from a dish of shrimp créole and smiled at Margaret.

"Mama thinks I am vain," she said. A slight tinge of defiance crept into the girl's voice as she added, "But —well, Mama buys me such beautiful clothes and always wants me to look nice, so it is difficult not to think about myself."

"But of course, *chérie,* you must look nice!" Madame Boré said. "Still, this does not mean that your needlework should be untidy nor that you may neglect your studies. Is this not so, Margaret, yes?"

Cécile's eyes were lowered, as if she expected Margaret to agree.

But Margaret did not want to alienate the charming girl. "It would be difficult for one so pretty not to think about herself," she said. "And I am sure Cécile will pay more attention to her studies when they become more meaningful."

Cécile's large heavily lashed eyes gazed gratefully at Margaret. "This is so," she said. "As for the needlework—well, my fingers do not seem to be made for stitching. Poor Sister Claire says I will never be a hemmer." Here, the girl sighed, but suddenly, her face lit up with high intention. "I know what I'll do," she went on excitedly, "I will make Margaret a piece of *petit point* for a purse. And you will see how neatly I can sew."

"Good," Madame Boré said. "You see! Margaret has already exerted her good influence."

Besides the family, there were a few young men of about Margaret's age, probably asked to make the evening more pleasant for her and for another young lady named Louise Catherine Jarbot. After an exquisite meal, the company went into the drawing room, a spacious salon furnished in Empire style, and containing beautiful pieces of imported bric-a-brac.

Cécile, seeming to sense Margaret's sudden pang of loneliness (for this lovely girl might have been her small Frances had she lived), moved up to Margaret's side.

"You'll see," she said. "I'll make you a beautiful piece of *petit point* for your purse."

She leaned over and kissed Margaret, then, evidently embarrassed by her own impulsiveness, hurried to join her mother on the other side of the room.

Louise Jarbot, sitting beside Margaret on a brocade settee, said softly, "How vulnerable the young are, and so wise."

When Margaret agreed, Louise Jarbot went on, still low-voiced and very sincere in her manner, "I hope you won't mind, but I feel I must say I've never met one who inspires me with so much admiration as you."

"Me!"

"Yes. One can feel without being told that your life is lived for others."

Margaret broke in, "But no! I merely find joy in ways that suit me. Others do the same, but their needs are different."

"I will not press the matter," Louise replied, "but —but if I can count you among my friends it would be a privilege."

Margaret was touched. Only in Sister Regis had she met a woman to whom she was drawn by some mysterious, unspoken bond. Miss Jarbot had the same warmth and candor as dear Sister Regis.

"It would make me very happy for us to be friends," Margaret told her.

Madame Boré then brought the conversation around to include the entire company by announcing that one of the young men, her protégé—a painter—had some things to say about his recent visit to Paris.

After a low murmur of agreement, the young man, Paul, said he had actually not spent so much time in Paris. "Because when I got there," he went on, "most of my friends had fled to Barbizon."

"But, why?" Madame Boré asked. "I cannot imagine artists leaving Paris."

"Ah, but now," Paul continued, "the masters are indulging in what they call 'romantic realism.' As you know, I wanted to study with Courbet, but he had joined Millet, Corot, and Rousseau in the village of Barbizon." The young man laughed. "It seems the human form is out of fashion, except as nymphs dancing in mossy glades, or peasants knee-deep in loam, and secondary to lush scenery. For myself, I will continue with more abstract daubing, and the world shall catch up with me!"

Then he went on to speak of music and literature, claiming that only the French mattered in the arts.

The other young man agreed. "The Germans are bombasts," he said. "I'm sure Mozart must have been injected with Gallic blood to have turned such graceful passages."

As Margaret listened, she felt how lacking was her knowledge in many areas, how limited her education. She knew people and had a good grasp of business now, but she'd never had the chance to catch up with the arts and letters. She would try—

But Louise Jarbot was speaking to her. "Such a lovely brooch, Margaret. Won't you tell us about it?" Margaret felt her face flushing. Sorry she was to have worn the brooch!

Louise Jarbot asked Margaret to tell her about her lovely brooch

Then remembering Sister Regis' words that belittling one's ancestry was another kind of pride, she told about the coat of arms, her mother's lineage dating back to that O'Rourke, Prince of Breffny, and ended with a wry remark: "And sure, if there is royal blood in our veins, it did not keep the line of ladies from spending most of their lives with scrubbing brush in hand."

"I always knew there was something special about you, Margaret," Madame Boré said. "It does not surprise me at all to find the skeleton of a prince hidden in your family closet."

"But more important," Louise Jarbot put in, "is Margaret's nobility of spirit."

Monsieur Boré, who had been quietly listening, said it was another phase of her personality that impressed him. "From what I have learned, you must be an excellent businesswoman. The success of your dairy is really astonishing. If you keep on this way, you will probably be the richest self-made woman in New Orleans." Though Margaret protested that her success was not yet very great, she admitted wanting to make a fortune which would enable her to provide for those in need. This led her to telling about the orphans and her hopes that they should soon have a home of their own.

"They are always likely to be put out by a landlord," she explained. "And I'm sure if someone would donate the ground, I will be able to manage the rest in not too many years."

"The Fortier family—" Madame Boré murmured, almost to herself.

"Who?" Margaret asked.

"Never mind, we shall see what we shall see," was the mysterious reply.

Margaret felt sure that her hostess had some plan in mind

to help forward her fondest dreams. And—the charming gay company receded, as she moved in fantasy through sunlit rooms and saw the pale faces of her orphans rounded and rosy with health, their clean calico dresses starched by extra help provided for the Sisters.

Then a shadow fell across her face as the light was blocked out by the artist's lean figure now standing close to her.

"So, may I have the pleasure of driving you home?"

Margaret started. "Yes, yes," she said. Before she had time to rise, two hands were clasping hers, and Louise Jarbot was saying softly, "Remember, we shall meet again. We are friends."

"Always," Margaret promised.

On the way home, she scarcely heard the pleasant chatter of her young Creole escort. He left her off at the old plantation house, and gallantly kissed her hand.

"Alas!" he murmured, "I feel that your mind is on more worthy matters than that of an admiring young man."

"Thank you, you have been very kind," Margaret said, then hurried into the house.

About a fortnight later Margaret received a letter from a solicitor saying that Madame Louise Fortier and her brother, Francis Saulet, would be willing to donate a lot on Camp Street for an orphanage, with the stipulation that within ten years the asylum and a chapel would be erected. Blithely Margaret's heart spoke before her head. Surely such a venture would not be impossible! Soon she would open her new dairy on Seventh Street. She could beg and borrow as she had done before. She would secure from Father Mullon and Monsieur Boré the names of wealthy people who might be interested in her cause. Yes, it could definitely be done!

One day, not long after, Sister Regis appeared waving a

letter in her hand and saying: "Margaret, what are we going to do?"

"Do, about what?"

"I have just received a letter. It states that this old DuBois plantation is going to be sold."

As she had done before, Margaret laughed. "It will always be the same unless we build an orphanage," she said.

"Build!"

"Yes," Margaret replied. "I've already been promised a site, if we can construct an orphanage and chapel within ten years."

"Oh, Margaret, the debts would be insurmountable!"

Margaret did become serious then. She knew that enormous funds would be required to complete the enterprise. Was she being a child, too impulsive and hasty? Something in her heart said, "no."

"This I can tell you, my dear Sister," she promised, "I will stand by you until the orphanage is free of all debts."

"That is enough for me, Margaret."

The decision made, Margaret's thoughts leaped into the further future. "And after this is done, we'll build a separate home for our infants—and after that—"

"Margaret, Margaret, Margaret," was all Sister Regis could say.

7

YOUR PEOPLE AND MY PEOPLE

When estimates came in for building the orphanage, they were so much more than she had imagined, Margaret was staggered. Still, she was determined to go on with the plans and by 1841, the new orphanage on Camp Street was completed. Although there were no landlords lurking in the background to evict at will the small community, enormous debts still hung over Margaret's head like the Sword of Damocles.

Finally, she decided to meet with Father Mullon and the Messrs. Bourke and Macready, to discuss ways and means of securing extra funds. As they sat around the rectory table, the men behaved as if she had been an irresponsible child.

Ignoring their patronizing attitude, Margaret said, "I've brought a statement with me." She snapped open a large black brocade handbag inset with a wide band of *petit point*, painstakingly stitched by Cécile Bore's patient, stubborn fingers. Her mother had been so delighted with the improved

Margaret met with her advisers to discuss was and means of securing funds

needlework, that instead of a small purse, she had had a good-sized bag made up and mounted as a gift for Margaret.

After placing some sheets of paper on the table, Margaret smiled, remembering what had been written on Cécile's card:

> *"Sister Claire said my progress is a miracle—that someday I might become a hemmer. Love, Cécile."*

Margaret was brought back to the present by the doleful clucking of Charles Macready's tongue. Both he and Nicholas Bourke were viewing the figures grimly.

Bourke was first to speak.

"Yes, Margaret," he said, "the orphanage is built. But, after looking over these figures, I'm afraid the sheriff will take it over. Or Madame Fortier might claim the value of the ground because her requirements will not have been met."

"I quite agree," Nicholas Bourke put in solemnly.

"—Because even though your dairies are doing well," Macready went on, "by no stretch of the imagination—not even your's—will you be able to finance this project alone within the next five years. You don't want the Sisters to be saddled with a heavy debt."

Since her fear that this might happen was the only reason Margaret had asked for the meeting, she spoke up now, a trifle sharply. "Certainly I don't want to leave the Sisters in debt. This is why I asked us to come together—to talk about ways of raising extra funds."

When she gazed appealingly at Father Mullon, he said, "As a rule, Margaret, I would think naught of appealing to my wealthy parishioners. Now, though, they all have the burden of building our new church. The architect's plans are very elaborate, and the Messrs. Dakin and Dakin have charged a pretty fee before one stone is set upon another. Now, of course, in my own mind there might be a question of whether it is more important to have someone like Léon Pomarède paint murals for our church at great expense or for such money be directed toward the poor. But such decisions are made by my trustees. I can do nothing about them."

"Of course I understand, Father!" Margaret said. "It is right and fitting that our church should be beautiful, and I would do everything possible to help make it so."

Father Mullon smiled. "There is no doubt about that, child," he told her. "You have already done more than your share."

"Well now," Charles Macready broke in, brisk and businesslike, "what about making a general public appeal?"

"You can put me down for the first contributor," Nicholas Bourke announced.

"Since the same was on my mind, I claim to be first," Macready said.

Father Mullon laughed, and said with pretended seriousness, "By the special authority invested in me by the Church, I pronounce you both to be first."

"Do you think the public will be interested in our orphans?" Margaret asked.

When her advisers still looked grim and doubtful, she turned to the priest and asked, "Isn't there a passage in the Scriptures, Father, about lilies in the field."

"And sure there is," Father Mullon answered.

Then he recited:

"Therefore I say to you, be not solicitous for your life,
what you shall eat, nor for your body, what you shall
put on. Is not the life more than the meat: and the body
more than the raiment? Behold the birds of the air,
for they neither sow, nor do they reap, nor gather into

*barns: and your heavenly Father feedeth them. Are not
you of much more value than they? . . . Consider the
lilies of the field, how they grow: they labour not, neither
do they spin. But I say to you, that not even Solomon
in all his glory was arrayed as one of these. ... Be not
therefore solicitous for tomorrow; for the morrow will
be solicitous for itself. Sufficient for the day is the evil
thereof."*

Father Mullon's voice was rich, melodic, and a brief silence
fell over his moved listeners.

Triumphantly, then, Margaret addressed the three. "So,
you see!"

"Yes," Father Mullon put in, "I do see. Perhaps we have
been fretting overmuch, and it is my intention to write to
some people I know, who have been generous to the poor. I
will explain about the deficit and say that you, Margaret, will
be happy to visit and tell them more if they are interested."

"Wouldn't it be better for you to make requests only in
your own name, Father?" Margaret asked. "No one would
recognize mine."

"You are wrong about that, child," Father Mullon told her.
"The name Margaret is a legend in New Orleans."

"Oh, come on with you, now, Father! You know there's no
need to bribe me with blarney to beg for the orphans."

Somehow the matter had been taken out of the realm
of reasonable judgment. Although there were no more
assurances than when they first sat down that the debts
could be paid, all now seemed convinced that Margaret
could manage.

After Father Mullon's letters had been sent, quite a few
small contributions came trickling in. In almost every case
Margaret's name was not only mentioned but there were

praises for her charity toward those of every color, class and creed.

Four of the wealthiest, most distinguished men of the city wrote of having heard of her good works, and they expressed a desire to meet her. One of these, Paul Tulane (who, for a man of his means gave away more money than anyone in the States—and by whose generosity Tulane University was to be brought into being), sent a sizable donation, saying that he would like to meet Margaret at a later date; business was taking him out of New Orleans for the next several months. Two of the others, John McDonogh and Judah Touro, asked if Margaret could call on them. A fourth, Thorny Lafon, wrote he had long wished to meet Margaret, and might he make an appointment to come to the orphanage?

Downright astonished she was, Margaret told Father Mullon, to be recognized by people of such importance. "Sure, it's little I've done of charity outside of helping the children," she said. "And this was charity to myself, because they gave me back love and a reason to be living."

Actually, Margaret did not recall or even consider her many acts of kindness, her impulsive generosity to all who asked for help.

"Even at the risk of giving you a swelled head," Father Mullon replied, "I must repeat, your name has become legend."

"Since it's not up to me to argue with the pastor," Margaret said, "would you, Father, set up appointments for me to meet these distinguished gentlemen."

Father Mullon said that he would. And one bleak day soon after, Margaret found herself on a small boat that shuttled across the river. On the other side, on his large plantation, lived John McDonogh. Margaret had heard that in spite of his millions, he was a cantankerous, eccentric gentleman; that, after having lived a gay and extravagant life in the city, he had come to prefer relative seclusion. So he had placed himself beyond the river and unwelcome company.

Margaret was a trifle nervous about this interview, and wondered why McDonogh wanted to see her. McDonogh, like herself, had lived in Baltimore before making his home in New Orleans, so she would remember this flimsy tie between them.

She was admitted to the house by a middle-aged Negro, who familiarly called out to his master, "John, the lady you was expecting is here."

Instead of the usual "Show her in," a querulous voice sounded from the shadows of the large drawing room, "Well, what is she waiting for?"

Margaret turned in the direction of the voice and started forward. Since the day was cloudy, it was difficult to see in that vast unlighted room. After brushing against a table, Margaret extended her hands, moving slowly like one blind. She inched her way toward the place from which she thought the voice had sounded.

It came again now, close by. "You're certainly taking your time, young lady."

This unreasonableness made her say rather tartly, "If I could see, I would come faster."

"No reason to burn oil unless I'm reading," was the crisp reply.

"No reason to break my neck, either!"

Heavenly saints! She shouldn't have said that! But the sound that followed was an unexpected laugh.

"I like spunk," Mr. McDonogh said. "It was not my intention for you to break your neck."

Now she could see his silhouette against a high-backed chair.

"From what I've been told, you've plenty of spunk yourself," Margaret returned.

"So you've heard about me," John McDonogh said. "No doubt that I'm a cranky, tight-fisted old man, without much sentiment." Here, he motioned her toward a chair and mumbled an apology about not rising. "Touch of the gout—anyhow, that's what my dratted doctor says. Bah! I eat like a Spartan, drink nothing but water, and have to pay out good money to the scoundrel who hides his stupidity behind the Hippocratic oath. I have no more gout than you, young lady."

"If you don't like your doctor, why don't you change him?" Margaret asked.

"None of them are any good," John McDonogh said. "Just like the clergy!"

"I gather then, Mr. McDonogh, you're not a Church man?"

"You gather correctly, young lady. But mind you, I'm no atheist—have deep respect for the Scriptures. But, when I look around at pious people, who think because they kneel in pews all of their pettiness and malice will be forgiven, it makes me sick. I suppose this shocks one of your Faith."

"No," Margaret said. "I can almost be agreeing with that. If one does not carry the lessons learned from the Church into the world, there's something lacking in one's understanding. But, Mr. McDonogh, are we not all sinners?"

"Yes, if you care to use that word," Mr. McDonogh said. "My quarrel with man is his villainous hypocrisy."

The bitterness in John McDonogh's voice suggested that this man had been very deeply hurt.

"Can it be," Margaret asked, "that one receives trust only when he gives it?"

Angrily he replied, "It can be the other way around. It can be that one extends his heart and trust, only to discover he is not valued for himself but for his money. Then, rejecting the idea of love, money and more money becomes the goal. This is my story, young lady, but do not look so alarmed. I have no real hate for my doctor, nor the clergy. I merely turn my own low self-esteem to the punishment of others."

"You didn't alarm me," Margaret said. "What you saw on my face was something else. It's an idealist you are, turned inside out from sorrow. And no matter if you like it or no, I shall keep you in my prayers."

"I guess prayers never hurt anyone," Mr. McDonogh said. "And, in my case, they will be a novelty. Much of my childhood was marred by the arguments of my Scotch and Irish parents about the proper way to save my soul. It made the idea of having one undesirable."

"What a pity," Margaret said.

"No, not at all, just one of the little accidents of birth. Now, *your* people—" He stopped short, then went on, "I will not make this distinction between us, Margaret. I would like to feel that in some areas we are of the *same* people. You and I both, at least, share concern over the fate of humanity.

"Now coming to the reason for your visit—mind you, the mere fact that children are parentless does not move me. In some instances I consider it an advantage. I did not intend to give you a donation. I was merely curious—but you brought me something, and John McDonogh always pays his debts."

Poor man, Margaret thought. Even in giving he tries to conceal he has a heart. But when McDonogh leaned forward extending a bill, his hand shook, and the expression on his face was kind.

"Oh, thank you, Mr. McDonogh!"

"Thank you, Margaret," he replied. His voice was very low, and in the now accustomed half-light, Mr. McDonogh was the abject picture of a lonely old man. Impulsively, Margaret leaned down and kissed him on the forehead.

When she told Father Mullon and her two advisers about her meeting with Mr. McDonogh, she received both teasing and approval. They said she must have charmed the old fellow, who rarely saw anyone. When he did, his visitors usually left in tears because of rough treatment by the miserly old man.

This was nonsense, Margaret told them. Anyone who could see beneath the surface would realize that Mr. McDonogh's hard exterior was merely a shell to cover up a tender heart.

"And don't let anyone be calling him a crank to me," was her final statement on that subject.

A few days later, she was ushered into the apartment of Judah Touro, adjacent to the place where he carried on his business. Unlike the dismal, shadowy drawing room of Mr. McDonogh, this one was flooded with sunlight that enhanced the beautiful Oriental rugs and multicolored bits of bric-a-brac, and transformed the bookshelves into a keyboard of tooled leather. Margaret had never seen so many books, and the idea of meeting the gentleman who read them made her a trifle fearful. But when Judah Touro came into the room, his smiling geniality at once put her at ease. He was slight and dapper and reminded her of the pure-blooded Spaniards still living in the Creole section.

Judah Touro must have read her mind, because he said, "No, I'm not Spanish. I come from Portugal, but then, I'm not sure that makes me a Portuguese. Because, you see, I am a Jew."

"Well," Margaret said, "I'm a Catholic, but since I come from Ireland, I'm Irish, too!"

"It is not quite the same," Mr. Touro said. "In Ireland a Catholic is welcome, but in Spain—no, not a Jew." His tones took on an edge of irony as he went on, "You, Margaret, in your innocence—because what I have heard of you denotes innocence—may not know that the first Spaniards in Louisiana had a Black Code. This, as you might suspect, did not refer to the Negro. No! The blacker one's skin, the better slave he'd make—so the brothers Lafitte and their fellow bandits made a fortune smuggling slaves into the country. But the Black Code excluded the entrance of Jews to the state. However, after a roundabout route through South America, some of us did manage to make our way here. The French were then in power and they are more lenient."

Dismayed, Margaret put in, "There is much trouble and suspicion between people, but surely in this enlightened age such things can't happen any more."

"Yes, they will happen," Judah Touro said sadly, "until enlightenment becomes that of the spirit as well as the intellect. Since you are such a person, Margaret, I asked you to call—to thank you in the name of my people."

"But—but I have done nothing—"

"You have but you don't remember," Mr. Touro said. "For many months you left milk at an old people's home, not asking about their faith or color; they were Jews. Then, there was that day when a gang of ruffians threatened an old man. They asked if he was dressed up for the Mardi Gras, because he wore the skullcap and beard of the Orthodox Jew. They tugged at his beard, might well have torn it off, if you, Margaret Haughery had not come along. My informant told me you scattered them with an umbrella. I doubt if you knew the old man was a Jew. You are good, Margaret."

"Never have I heard such nonsense," Margaret said.

"Making it a virtue to come to the aid of an old man! You have a poor opinion of people, Mr. Touro."

"Not really," the man replied. "But a good opinion of very few."

"Heavenly saints!" Margaret said, "it's only lately I've been hearing so much about 'your people, and my people.' Here in America, it's about time to be thinking of *our* people."

"Someday, maybe," Judah Touro said. "But not before much bloodshed and sorrow."

After a brief silence, Margaret spoke about his beautiful apartment, especially mentioning Mr. Touro's many books.

"Yes," he said, "I love to read, especially in French. Stendahl, Hugo, and Balzac are my friends, especially Balzac, whose *Human Comedy* puts people in their proper place, suggests their unimportance."

"I wish I had more time to read and learn things," Margaret said. "There's so much I don't know."

"There is nothing *important* you do not know," Mr. Touro replied.

After they had chatted for a while, Mr. Touro gave Margaret a large donation for the orphanage.

"Oh, thank you!" Margaret said.

"No, I thank you, Margaret. You are one of the few who 'do not your justice before men, to be seen by them.' "

A little surprised, Margaret asked, "Are those words also in your Bible?"

"No. I, too, find the words of Christ extremely beautiful."

They shook hands and promised to meet again.

Of the three who had asked to meet Margaret, only Thorny Lafon now remained. Soon after, however, he did come to the orphanage, a soft-voiced Negro with the gentlest expression Margaret had ever seen. He, too, told of having heard of her good works for his people, and explained that since it was his privilege to be a free man, he also tried to be of service to others.

"I am only in my early thirties," he said, "but I have in a small way been successful." He went on to explain that what he wanted for his people was education, so that, when they were free, they would be able to recognize true friends and not believe the false promises of those who would exploit them.

"For my people will be free," he said. "Now, they are like children. And who can blame them for their voodoo dances, their *gris-gris*—"

When Margaret looked puzzled, he went on to explain that the *gris-gris* was a charm, a talisman worn for luck or to conjure evil upon one's enemies.

"It is no wonder that the Congo customs remain," he said, "when people are owned and subject to the wills of others. Someday it will be different, but first the slave will have to believe in his own dignity; this will take time and education."

His words sent tears to Margaret's eyes. Noticing them, Thorny Lafon said impulsively, "I fear I have been rude. It was for *you* I came, not to unload my own beliefs and burdens."

"Your humility shames me," Margaret said.

"If I have such a quality," Thorny Lafon replied, "it is surely a bond we share."

He gave her a contribution for the children, and, after apologizing that it could not be more, went away.

Instead of going to the children, Margaret threw a shawl around her shoulders and put on her little bonnet. Numbed by sorrow, she seemed not to be walking of her own will, but wandering about in a dream. Her legs, though, followed the direction she must take, and soon she was kneeling before the altar at St. Patrick's. Head lowered to her hands, she felt hot tears trickle through her fingers.

"Dear God," she prayed, "please let people come together in love. Help them see this is the only way."

Over and over she said the same. Gradually the answer came: "Be patient, Margaret, for the patient shall inherit the land."

Her spirits were lightened; it would take long; but someday, under God, brotherhood would triumph over fear and suspicion.

8

SHADOWS OVER NEW ORLEANS

By 1845, the orphanage was incorporated under the name of St. Therese's Asylum. And during the next five years, in spite of dire predictions, all debts were paid. The home and the chapel were standing and clear, a monument to Margaret's toil and energy.

One accomplishment behind, there remained another goal to be fulfilled—her Baby House. St. Therese was crowded to capacity; almost every year, and usually following some such catastrophe as a flood or epidemic, many children were left parentless and without homes. Always at the orphanage it was, "Let's try to push the cots closer together, try to make room for more," and crowding made it impossible to have separate quarters for the babies. Their innocence, their helplessness, never failed to strike a chord in Margaret's heart. For every ill and fretful infant was a poignant reminder of little Frances, lifeless in her arms.

To provide for others in the way she wished, meant that

more and more of Margaret's time was taken up in supervising her dairies, and less with the children; she missed those warm, close contacts. At first her services had been required for domestic chores: feeding the children, sewing and lending a hand when they were ill. Now, she had to admit, the need for her presence was not so great as was raising funds for the orphans' future security. The home could now afford extra help for the Sisters, and Margaret's role had become more that of provider than of one who tended the children. Actually she would rather have been the tender. But what was best for the children's welfare, that she must be!

Because her dairies functioned better when under her constant supervision, Margaret had in mind to move uptown where she would be closer to them. However, to tell Sister Regis that after fifteen years she meant to make a change required all of Margaret's resourcefulness. Because if she did not make it seem that leaving was what she herself most desired, Sister Regis would insist that she stay.

One evening after the children were asleep, she and her friend sat discussing a boy recently admitted to the orphanage. Poverty and the sudden recent death of his parents had caused this youngster to erect a wall of defiance to hide his sorrow. He was quite unmanageable, and had become a swaggering bully to make himself feel important.

"Why don't *you* have a talk with him, Margaret?" Sister Regis asked. "You have such a way with unhappy children."

Now was good a time as any to tell her news, Margaret thought. She did promise to talk to *this* boy, but went on to say that many of the Sisters could handle children better than she—that, indeed, since most of her time was taken up with business matters, she had lost much of her touch with youthful thinking.

"This is nonsense, and you know it, Margaret," Sister Regis said. "No one understands the children better than you. Are you trying to tell me something else?"

"Yes," Margaret said, "I have recently considered moving uptown."

"Moving!"

Sister Regis' expression of sorrow made it difficult to speak, but Margaret went on, "I do believe, Sister, the dairies need my eye on them constantly, and it has been my idea to find a home near Seventh Street."

"Have you no regrets about leaving us?" Sister Regis' voice was very low.

And Margaret discovered she could not pretend with her friend; tears came to her eyes and she could scarcely answer. "Oh, yes, Sister. The thought of leaving fills me with sadness, but let's be sensible. Let's think for a moment only what's best for the children. You know how overcrowded we are now, how much it would mean to have a Baby House."

"I can't consider only the children, Margaret, but also you," Sister Regis replied. "It will not be the same here without you."

The Sister's voice choked with emotion. So rarely did she reveal her feelings that to gaze at her now was almost more than Margaret could bear. Still in the following silence she held to her resolution.

"I will be visiting here often, Sister," she said. "You have always known of my dream to make myself rich so I can give to others."

Sister Regis nodded. "But," she said, "as I told you long ago, Margaret, your wonderful influence is more important than any worldly goods. I still feel this. The Baby House can wait."

"I suppose it can," Margaret agreed. "But, in truth, isn't it more important for the babies to have their home than for me to remain here?"

Now, the silence was longer than before. It was finally broken by Sister Regis. "I have to admit, Margaret," she said, "that in weakness I was thinking of myself. We have been friends together for so long—"

"Our friendship can't be weakened by mere distance," Margaret said. "Indeed, I believe it will endure forever."

"I am certain this is so," Sister Regis said.

Then, since the matter was decided, both assumed an attitude of gaiety, aiming to raise the other's spirit.

One evening, not long after she had moved, Monsieur and Madame Boré stopped before Margaret's tiny new home. They were on their way to Cécile's graduation exercises. Cécile had sent Margaret a short, intense little note urging her to come. She wrote:

> *"Dear Margaret: You* must *be present! My life is in such a tangle, graduation means nothing to me. I* must *speak to you.*
>
> Love, Cécile.

Margaret had watched the lovely child Cécile grow into young womanhood, with wide, brown, heavily-lashed eyes, a flawless complexion and a beautiful curve of lips, which, when she was disturbed, took on a look of pouting. Cécile moved gracefully and held high her head, topped with a halo of auburn curls. From the first, Margaret had been a confidante, a kind of older sister to the child, a status that still endured. While fastening her brooch, Margaret wondered what kind of scrape or problem had caused the dramatic tone of Cécile's note.

Besides Monsieur and Madame Boré, she found Louise Jarbot also waiting in the carriage. Although usually present on family occasions, Paul the painter was not with them that evening. He was no longer Madame Boré's young protégé, but a man in his late thirties, acclaimed by his *avant garde* artist friends as a genius.

Seated beside her friend Louise, Margaret felt a kind of tension in the air. Madame Boré seemed particularly disturbed. On such occasions she usually enlivened the company with her gay conversation, but this time, after greeting Margaret with a wan " *'ello, chérie,*" she slipped back into silence. It was Monsieur Boré who took on the duties of host and spoke about happenings of the day.

"By the way, Margaret," he said, "have you heard about John McDonogh's death?"

"No! When did it happen?"

"Almost a fortnight ago. His will was probated today. He left millions to the Public Schools of New Orleans and Baltimore."

"Poor lonely man!" Margaret said. "I doubt there were many loving him but his slaves. He was good to them—wanted them to be free."

"Most considered him an eccentric," Monsieur Boré said, "but I imagine his enormous bequests will do much to alter public opinion."

"Little that helps to ease his past loneliness," Margaret remarked.

This was followed by silence; all one heard were horses' hoofs striking against the cobblestones.

Finally Madame Boré gave a deep sigh and said, "Yes, life is full of unhappiness." She leaned forward and touched

Margaret's arm with the tip of her long, suede gloves. "I know," she went on, "you had a note from Cécile. She told me, and that she intends to speak to you privately. Though I do not wish to sway your advice to her, I can't believe it unfair to explain my own point of view."

She was so intense and unlike herself that Margaret was alarmed.

"Cécile isn't in any serious trouble?" she asked.

"Not in the ordinary sense," Madame Boré told her. "But to me—she is dooming herself to a terrible fate."

Madame Boré took from her handbag a miniature square of fine linen surrounded by a wide border of real lace. With this weblike kerchief she daubed her pretty eyes.

Her husband leaned toward her and spoke in soothing tones, "You are taking this matter too seriously, my dear."

Instead of being comforted, his wife's voice tilted high in annoyance. "You see! You are taking sides with Cécile again."

"It is not that, only there's no reason to worry at this time."

"No reason!" Madame Boré then spoke directly to Margaret. "You know how fond we all are of Paul. Well—for years it 'as been accepted that Cécile would marry him. He adores her, and our families have looked forward to this alliance with hope and happiness. Now, Margaret, it may seem strange to you that marriages should be arranged, but with us it is quite customary. Often such alliances work out better than the decision of impulsive young people. Oh, dear! I can see by your expression, you do not agree with me!"

"Well, now," Margaret said, "I imagine some such marriages may turn out very well. But if Cécile has been brought up with the idea of marrying Paul, why does she object now?"

"Why, why?" Madame Boré cried. "The silly child thinks

she has fallen in love with the brother of one of her classmates. He's probably an American, with one of those hideous houses in the Garden District. Oh, everyone is against me! What am I going to do?"

"Believe me, I am not against you," Margaret said. "It is only that I loved my husband and can't imagine anything worse than being married to one and yearning for another."

Louise, whose tender heart always made her consider everyone in a situation, asked gently, "What about Paul?"

"He will be 'eartbroken," Madame Boré cried.

Her husband disagreed. "I think you exaggerate this, my dear. Paul is like one of the family. He is fond of Cécile, but I believe his admiration for you is no less. Paul is a man partially wedded to his art; I do not think he will greatly suffer."

"If it is not bold, I would like to know," Margaret said, "was your own marriage arranged?"

"In a way, yes," Madame Boré said. "Though I always loved Jacques—and I think—"

"You do not 'think,' you *know*!" Here Monsieur Boré secured his wife's gloved hand and clasped it tightly.

"I *do* know. Yes, I must admit our marriage was one of love."

They were now nearing the Ursuline Convent where the ceremonies were to take place. This order of nuns were the earliest educators in the Colony. Indeed, theirs was the only teaching institution in New Orleans when it was started by six Ursulines and two Jesuits who had arrived there in 1727. Their original convent was the oldest building in the city, having been spared in a fire that practically wiped out the entire settlement in 1788.

From their windows, a succession of cloistered nuns had

gazed upon a historic panorama of change. Nearby, in the Place d'Armes, four flags had been unfurled before their eyes. First, that of France to be replaced by the Spanish flag, then later the tricolor of the French Republic. And, after the annexation of Louisiana to the States, the Stars and Stripes fluttered on the flagpole.

Equal in strength and gentleness were these women, who could do the most menial tasks and also train gauche little girls to become charming, literate young ladies. Their charges, now seated on a raised platform, dressed in modest white hand-tucked frocks, were like a spray of lovely lilies.

None, however, were quite so beautiful as Cécile. But she was pale, and Margaret thought that in spite of the rounded curve of her cheeks, her wide-eyed candor, her expression of sadness made Cécile seem older than the others.

The ceremonies were simple, starting with a prayer. After this, each of the young ladies recited a small piece, all with bell-toned, perfect diction, whether in French or English. Cécile read from Longfellow's "Evangeline" of those Acadian refugees from Nova Scotia who had been expelled by the British and arrived in New Orleans in 1765. Even her voice took on the quality of sharing the frightening experiences of wandering people. When she was seated again, Cécile's clasped hands were tense, rigid balls.

When the ceremonies were over, each graduate was given her diploma, then went from the platform to receive congratulations from her family. Cécile joined her father and mother and Louise and Margaret, and accepted their best wishes with a forced and fleeting smile.

As they stood talking together, a classmate came up, followed by her elder brother. Cécile introduced them as Jane and—and George Adams. The brief, tender smile she directed toward the young man left no doubt he was the one who had turned her heart from Paul.

Jane's outgoing chatter did little to thaw the frigid atmosphere. "Now remember, Cécile, you promised we will see one another often," she said. "I would just die if we did not get together—"

Cécile agreed, and as the two talked about future plans, George, armed with a charming smile and perfect manners, squarely faced Cécile's mother. "I am glad to have this opportunity to meet you, Madame Boré," he said. "I want your permission to call on Cécile." When it seemed for a moment she was not going to answer, Cécile's face grew pale and she placed a trembling hand on Margaret's arm. Finally, Madame Boré replied, "Yes, of course," but with such reluctance that the words were obviously forced from her only by good manners.

Monsieur Boré said more cordially, "We shall be happy to have you call, George, and you, too, Jane." Cécile tucked her arm within the crook of Margaret's as they went to the waiting carriage. After they were all seated, she burst into unrestrained sobs. "My graduation was the most unhappy day of my life," she cried. "Mama was rude. I *will* see George, no matter what anyone says!"

At this, her mother also wept. "What about Paul?" she asked. "No one is thinking about Paul."

"I have already spoken to him," Cécile announced. "Because Paul is gallant, he pretended to be heartbroken. But after we spoke for a while, he said I would always be his adorable little sister, and you and Papa his most valued friends."

"You have done this without consulting me!"

"Certainly. I had no wish to deceive Paul, but I cannot

marry him." Cécile then turned to Margaret and added imploringly, "You understand; please explain to Mama."

"I already have," Margaret told her truthfully. "I believe in love, but you are young Cécile. Don't be hasty in making up your mind."

"I won't," Cécile promised. "I shall never marry against my parents' wishes, no matter how I suffer." After this sad little declaration, the journey was made in silence, and the rumble of wheels on the cobblestones sounded very loud.

Water was the reason for New Orleans, that cypress swamp which had gradually become a city. In the outlying undrained areas, wild trees, shrubs, grasses, herbs throve in mossy bogs. Live oaks, heavy with Spanish moss, rose in palmetto thickets; tall cypress trees gazed down on swampland dotted with lavender hyacinth floats, irises, lily ponds, and vines tooting their orange-colored trumpets. Into the lake and river flowed a network of waterways, where the bayou folk paddled their cypress-hewn pirogues to go fishing, shopping or even pay social calls.

Then there was the river, with floating palaces ever becoming more elaborate. Nothing was more fashionable than a season in New Orleans, the most sophisticated city in America. Where else in the States could one so well show off jewels, costumes and accessories as at the opera in New Orleans? Where, for that matter, could one purchase more magnificent hand-wrought jewelry, more enticing perfumes and cosmetics than in that delightful frivolous city at the river's mouth?

Yes, the Mississippi was New Orleans' darling, on whose crest came ever more prosperity. The Erie Canal —*poof!*Why, it had not made a dent in transportation! As for those stupid engines with steam spouting from their funneled stacks—who would ever want to travel by railroad!

It seemed that nothing would ever halt that spiraling upward trend of gaiety, which reached its climax at the Mardi Gras. Celebrated on the day before Ash Wednesday, processions of people paraded the streets in beautiful or grotesque costumes, some on horseback, some in open carriages. Animal headdresses, fauns and nymphs reminded that the "carnival" dated back to Roman and pagan festivities. Clowns mingled with kings and Indians; music ran the gamut from plantation airs and West Indian nonsense lyrics to the more sedate ditty of the day. Since frivolity was the rule, the carnival must be intoxicating, hilarious! All was always well in New Orleans, except—

Except—people did not like to speak of them, the plagues, the hurricanes. How dare outsiders call their lovely city, "the graveyard of the nation"? In their pride, the citizens of New Orleans called yellow fever a "stranger's disease," and statistically had proof on their side. The cause of the fever and methods of its prevention were little known, but it had been established that of those stricken the largest percentage were either strangers or people who had not lived long in the city.

Margaret, who as a child had lost both parents and a younger brother in a yellow fever epidemic in Baltimore, had subsequently been exposed again and again to the disease. In every epidemic she had nursed the sick, visited the homes of those stricken, cared for the children and in many cases brought back the parentless to the orphanage. Because of her continuous contacts, it could have been that she was immune to the dread disease, which called for her supreme endurance during the plague in 1853.

Rain fell for three whole days and nights, and the air had an oppressive quality that made it hard to breathe. One evening, as she came home from the dairy, Margaret was met by her frightened maid, Clothilde, who said Father Mullon had sent a message for her to join him at the rectory as soon as possible.

The boy who had brought the message told of having seen on his way three strapping men drop dead in their tracks!

"Now, don't be too upset, Chloe," Margaret told the panic-stricken girl. "We've had these epidemics before."

"I'll try, Miss Margaret," her maid replied. "You go change from your wet clothes and I'll fetch you a bit of dinner before you leave."

While Margaret was eating, an anxious Louise Jarbot came to add what she had learned. It seemed there had been many cases of the fever during the past week. But the authorities, thinking perhaps the plague could be kept under control, had made no public announcements. Now, however, the situation had gotten out of hand, and all available health agencies were being mustered into service. People were swarming out of the city in every conceivable way.

"Lawdy, Lawdy!" Chloe moaned.

"Don't worry too much," Louise Jarbot put in to reassure her, "every method will be tried to keep the disease from spreading."

Prophetically her words were followed by the sound of cannon fire somewhere in the city. This was repeated, then again. Somehow, this noise brought some faint comfort to the listeners, because it was then believed that explosions had the power to confine the ravages of yellow fever.

After the boom died out, Margaret said, "I'm going to the rectory. Maybe I can help visiting the sick."

"I am going with you," Louise Jarbot said.

"No, absolutely no, Louise." Margaret spoke very firmly. "You are delicate and there are other things you can do. For instance, if you would take a message to my foreman at the dairy, it would be very helpful. Tell him that anyone not feeling well must remain at home, and if any of the workers need my help he should send for me at once."

"I will do what you say, Margaret," Louise replied, "but I intend to stay here until the plague is over—see that you get some sleep and eat properly."

After Margaret agreed to this, she called to her coachman that she was ready and started on her way. Large vehicles were now spreading tar over the city streets. Soon, this thick, black substance would be ignited, because of folklore claiming that fumes and flames also helped stem the tide of infection. As they drove along, Margaret saw a man stagger and fall heavily onto the ground.

"Stop!" she bid her coachman, then got out of the carriage and bent over the stricken man. Turning, she beckoned the driver to join her.

Despite the reluctance of the frightened man, together they carried the victim into her carriage, and Margaret directed that he be taken to a small hospital a few blocks away. When they arrived, it seemed at first the place was totally deserted, except for corpses lying in the corridor. From a wing, however, she heard sounds of moans and voices. Hastening there, Margaret saw a small ward of beds containing victims in varying stages of the horrible disease. Though most of the personnel had fled, a doctor was in attendance and also a man of the cloth. At first Margaret thought him to be a priest, but he was Reverend Theodore Clapp, a Presbyterian minister, whose charitable self- sacrifice made him beloved of

Margaret bent over the man stricken with yellow fever

all New Orleans. The minister admitted having had certain preconceived prejudices toward the Roman Church and its clergy when he had come to the city. But during the yellow fever epidemic of 1832, he had remained in New Orleans and it was then, he said, "that I had no coadjutors but the Roman Catholic priests." These, he had found to be cultured, charitable gentlemen, now counted among his most devoted friends.

He had met Margaret before in times of tribulation, and now, gazing up from a man writhing in convulsions, the minister asked, "What are you doing here, Margaret?"

She explained how, on her way to Father Mullon, she had picked up a sick man on the street. "But," said Margaret, "there are none to carry him in. When my coachman saw the bodies downstairs, he fled in terror to the carriage."

When this was related to the doctor, he asked if the patient was still alive.

"He was when I left."

Together Reverend Clapp and the doctor went to the street; but, since they found the man had died, they left his body in the corridor with the others.

After returning to the ward, the minister said to Margaret, "The cart will soon be along."

This grim vehicle would rumble along the cobblestones until the plague was over, the driver calling out in mournful tones, "Bring out your dead. Bring out your dead. . . ."

"Since you were on your way to Father Mullon," Dr. Clapp said, "do not let me detain you, Margaret."

"There could be no need greater than you have here," she answered. "There will be other times for me to help Father Mullon."

For weeks Margaret labored almost beyond endurance, first here, then there, tending the sick, comforting the bereaved. Life became a hideous blur, with the constant sounds of cannon, nights lit up like day from the burning tar when windows revealed a panorama of death and suffering. Eight thousand people perished of yellow fever during that epidemic of 1853.

One evening, when Margaret arrived home dog-tired, Louise agitatedly greeted her at the door. Usually she insisted that Margaret eat and take a rest, but now Louise could not conceal her frightening news. Madame Boré's coachman had been there, saying that Cécile was very ill and asking to see Margaret.

"Is it the plague?"

Louise said she didn't know. The family had been unable to get a doctor; one was expected soon.

At once Margaret started for the Boré home, terrified at the idea that the child Cécile might be stricken, dying. But— Cécile was no child; she was a young woman, who, during the past few years had matured because of sadness. For, in spite of George's constancy, Cécile would not marry him without her mother's consent, and Madame Boré had stubbornly held to her objections. Now, though, when Margaret entered the house, she was greeted by a frantic mother who burst out that she would, if only God spared her daughter, do "anything— anything to atone for foolish pride."

"Go to her, Margaret," Madame Boré implored. "You have seen much of this terrible disease. Tell me, tell me the truth about what you think."

Cécile was flushed and seemed quite feverish, but after seeing her, Margaret could state honestly that according to her experiences with plague, Cécile had none of the usual symptoms. "But this is only my view," Margaret went on. "When do you expect the doctor?"

He was due at any moment, they told her.

Soon the front door knocker sounded. It was not the doctor but George Adams, who pushed past the servants, mounted the steps two at a time and unceremoniously rushed into the sickroom.

"Cécile!"

"George!"

He was across the room, seated on the edge of her bed, and clinging to Cécile's hands.

She drew back, saying, "You must not come close to me, George. I may have the fever."

"If you do, then I will have it, too!" he cried. "I can no longer go on in life without you."

These words, worthy of the most romantic and ardent Creole, caused Madame Boré to gaze down at them with a smile that bestowed her blessing.

Soon after this the doctor arrived and the verdict he gave was of the best: Cécile did not have the yellow fever. Although she was very ill, her ailment was not dangerous.

Then, suddenly one day, after a storm dispelled the fog and oppressive atmosphere, no more people were stricken with the plague.

Cécile was soon restored to health and when banns for their marriage were published, she said to Margaret, "May I name my first daughter after you—and will you be her godmother?"

There was nothing, Margaret said, that would make her happier.

9
THE BREAD WOMAN

After the epidemic of 1853, the Baby House became an absolute necessity. No matter how close cots were moved together, or by what makeshift arrangements orphaned children found shelter at St. Therese's Asylum, there was not enough room. This time, when Margaret decided to go ahead with plans to build, there were no dissenting voices among her advisers.

Within a few years, a monument arose on the corner of Magazine and Race Streets, born through love of a mother whose arms had been made empty by the death of her baby girl. The loss of her own parents at an early age had given Margaret a premature knowledge of separation from loved ones. Later, Charles and little Frances had held out hope that she could live with love again. Charles died; but there was little Frances, that all-meaningful bond between them. When this tie, too, was severed, all seemed lost. But her Faith had dealt with time, transforming past loneliness into a present testimonial. It rose, Margaret's Baby House, where every infant would receive the best of care in clean, uncrowded, sunlit rooms. Limitless little Franceses, slumbering in their cribs!

It was the year 1859, a mild clear day, when Margaret was driven to a small studio in the French Quarter. She had often been asked to sit for a portrait, but she had refused, saying that the idea of having her likeness made was blithering nonsense. However, the trustees of the orphanage had asked so often for her portrait, Margaret finally decided to sit. Paul, the Boré's friend had advised her to go to a young artist, a pupil of Léon Pomarède who had painted the murals in St. Patrick's Cathedral. Paul said he would like to have painted the portrait himself, but his abstract treatment of the human form would probably bring down the wrath of the trustees and frighten the little children.

To which Margaret replied laughingly, "Go 'long with you! It would take more than your talent to make an abstract out of my substantial frame."

So she'd gone to the young man Paul recommended and her portrait was almost completed. Since she had mentioned never feeling at ease in anything but her bonnet and shawl, this was what she wore. The first few sittings were unsuccessful because, no matter how she tried, Margaret felt her face freezing into an expression of self-consciousness.

"Relax," the artist told her, "talk, tell me about yourself."

When Margaret spoke, especially of the children, the young man said, "I know what we need to make you feel at home."

He'd left the room and gone into a courtyard, where Margaret heard him shout, "I want to borrow a couple of children—anywhere between the ages of four and seven."

In a matter of minutes, several bedraggled recruits poured into the studio, all claiming the privilege of posing. With the children close by, Margaret's face had relaxed in a sweet, motherly expression.

Since this was her final sitting, she had brought clothes and toys for these children who by posing supplemented the income of their needy families. After they had gone, Margaret gave the artist money for their families, and took a last look at the portrait before it would be delivered.

"A fine painting it is, to be sure," she said, "but haven't you rid me of my plainness?"

"Quite the contrary," the artist replied. "My problem was to capture both the strength and spirituality in your face, and the task has been most challenging."

"Blarney!" Margaret exclaimed. "But, usually avoiding mirrors, I am not too familiar with my face."

The artist smiled and said, "I wish some of my other patrons would do the same, since they complain I have not seen what they see in their mirrors. But I do hope, Margaret, you like the portrait."

"I do. I like it very much."

Before returning home, Margaret decided to stop at the Baby House. On her way, she drove by a public school, newly erected through the generosity of John McDonogh, past the Touro Synagogue and Infirmary, reminding her of the recent death of Judah Touro whose bequests to every kind of charity challenged that he had ever used the phrase, "my people."

She was greeted at the door of the Baby House by a young nun, who announced excitedly that Margaret had a visitor. The Sisters had been trying to get in touch with her all afternoon. It was obvious from the novice's manner that this guest was someone special. Indeed, she behaved like one trying to soften a shock.

At once Margaret suspected. For the past years, she had been exchanging letters with her brother John, who had come from Ireland to make his home in Baltimore. In spite of their correspondence, she felt a sense of unreality about a relationship broken when she was merely a child of five. She remembered well the brothers and sisters left behind, but since there had been no contact since, time had dimmed her sense of belonging to a family.

Still not entirely sure it was he, she asked, "My brother?"

"Yes. The minute I set my eyes on him, I knew. He is very like you."

"Where—?"

"I made him comfortable in the Trustees Room, Margaret."

Heart thumping, Margaret opened the door. When her brother turned, it was obvious that he, too, felt shy and strange about their meeting.

"Margaret!"

"John!"

Slowly the distance between them shortened; their hands met. Then as they gazed into each other's face, their similarity of expression caused both to burst into peals of laughter. They embraced, and after the laughter there came tears and questions—and more questions aimed at pushing back time to the day of their parting.

Margaret learned that her other brothers and sisters had been raised by an Uncle O'Rourke who loved them and brought them up as if they were his own; that John was married to a charming young woman named Mary, had children and a thriving business in Baltimore.

"But now, you, Margaret?"

Briefly she sketched in her life, unable to give more than a childlike, confused impression of their parents' death. She spoke of Charles and the baby Frances—here she wept—and of what had happened since then. Margaret's recitation made it seem that her own life was little different than the mundane existence of most.

"But I hear that you're the most important woman in New Orleans," John said.

"You'll never be getting a straight picture of me from the Sisters," Margaret told him.

Then she asked her brother how long he intended to remain in New Orleans.

"After the little I've seen of this lovely city, I should like to remain in it forever," he said. "The climate is so fair, so balmy—and since one of our daughters is extremely frail, I've been wondering if she might fare better here."

"No," Margaret said firmly, "No. I thought the same about Charles, that he would be cured. But, let us go now, John; my carriage is waiting."

Margaret told her coachman to stop at the D'Aquin bakery on New Levee Street before taking them to her home. "They have the most delicious bread in New Orleans," she explained. "Monsieur D'Aquin has always been so generous to my orphans. Recently his business has been falling off, so I loaned him money to put him on his feet again."

"Business is also unsettled up North," John Gaffney told his sister. "Perhaps because of so much talk about trouble between the North and South."

Margaret sighed. "These rumors worry me," she replied, "but I can't believe these differences will not be reconciled."

"I hope you're right," her brother said. "There's great resentment against slavery in the North, and against the South's unwillingness to cooperate with the Federal Government. I sometimes think if these matters are not soon adjusted we may have civil war."

"Not that!" Margaret exclaimed. "I pray this great country will never be divided!"

"Perhaps it will not happen," John said.

The carriage came to a halt in front of the bakery. When they entered, Monsieur D'Aquin greeted Margaret warmly. On meeting her brother he said, "Margaret is a remarkable woman. I am greatly in debt to her.

Indeed, she now owns even more stock in the bakery than I. It would be to the benefit of both if she would buy me out."

"Come now, my friend," Margaret said, "we have often spoken of this before. What do I know about running a bakery?"

"What did you know about running a dairy before you started?" Monsieur D'Aquin asked.

Margaret laughed. "My two cows were willing partners in that deal," she said. "And now, Monsieur D'Aquin, will you let us have some of your delicious bread and rolls. Hospitality to my brother would be lacking unless I served them."

During the next few days, Margaret showed her brother around the city. No matter where they went, whether in the Garden District, the section where stately white-pillared homes flaunted their owner's prosperity in cotton or sugar cane, or in the French Quarter, Margaret was affectionately greeted by many people.

She took John to the French Market, where along with exotic foods, birds and flowers, the Choctaw and Chitimacha Indians sold their reed-caned baskets. Margaret bought one of the largest, saying she intended to fill it with gifts for her new-found family in Baltimore! She selected fabrics for dresses and toys for the children, and an enameled brooch for the sister-in-law she had never seen.

The brother and sister went to Mass at St. Patrick's, where they lingered after the service so that John could meet her beloved Father Mullon. Happy he was, the priest said, to know Margaret had a man in the family who could be called upon when his willful sister needed to be taken in hand. He went on, then, warmly extolling Margaret's charity, which was of an order "encompassing true love and humility."

Rarely concluding anything without a laugh, however, Father Mullon added, "But along with these saintly virtues, our Margaret has some very worldly traits. Once, she sought financial advice, but now others consult her. Indeed, it has come to my ears that she intends to deprive poor Monsieur D'Aquin of his bakery."

When Margaret put in, "If I do, it will not be because I want to," Father Mullon became serious again.

"To buy out his business might be an advantage to both, Margaret," he said.

After Margaret said she would consider the matter carefully, she and John went out to the waiting carriage.

On the way home, her brother again spoke of the bakery. He said he believed Margaret might be making an excellent investment if she put her money into such a venture. Because, he explained, womanly intuition would be an asset in any business dealing with food; he would advise her not to treat the offer lightly.

"I would have to sell my dairies," Margaret told him. "They now take up most of my time." Silent for a moment, she went on, "I don't want to be wealthy, John, but keeping up the things I've started takes most of my present income. There is still so much I want to do. If I thought the bakery would hasten those ends—well, I would change from milkmaid to bread woman."

Then there came into her mind the words, "Give us this day our daily bread," and suddenly she wanted to be an instrument of God, helping in a small way to make this prayer come true. She would sell her dairies, and take over the bakery!

It had been her hope to have a small gathering of friends to meet her brother, but on arriving home there was a letter from Baltimore urging John to return at once; his daughter was gravely ill. Although their time together had been too brief, both held to the happy knowledge that an ocean no longer lay between them. But, after John had gone, Margaret thought again of their talk about a possible war. If it came, it would cut a chasm across the country, more cruelly dividing them than the most turbulent of seas.

Margaret fretted about the sick little niece she had never seen. However, after a few weeks, a letter arrived saying that the child was well again; an incorrect diagnosis had caused the false alarm. Mary, her sister-in-law, also enclosed a note, thanking Margaret for her lovely gifts and expressing the hope that before long they would all get together.

The idea of purchasing the bakery remained in Margaret's mind. She'd received word from Monsieur D'Aquin that business had become so bad he might have to go into bankruptcy. She decided to visit him again and discuss serving an apprenticeship with him before signing the final papers of purchase.

During their talk, Monsieur D'Aquin explained every detail of the business: where he bought his flour, how he kept his books, and his problems concerning the distribution of his bread. As he spoke, it seemed to Margaret that the man had in some ways been too conservative, not used the proper means to promote his goods. With such a stable commodity, even unsettled times should not so greatly have affected his business. The more Margaret listened, the more she became convinced of her ability to make the bakery into a growing concern, after a period of learning. This, she would start at once.

From previous experience, she knew success would depend upon her personal attention. So she gave up her small house and moved with her maid Chloe to the apartment above the bakery. How curious that she should again be living on New Levee Street, not far from the site of Old Withers! But the neighborhood had gradually changed, as had all others since 1852, when, after sixteen years of tripartite government, the city was reunited into a single municipality. Racial distribution was far less fixed, and along with the Irish, there were German, Slavic, and even French names of newcomers.

Because of many tastes, Margaret thought it wise to include a more varied assortment of foodstuffs in her bakery. Soon, along with the delicious brown loaves of French bread, her stock included cakes, cookies and macaroni, all of which were in great demand. It was not long before she had built up a sizeable marine trade, and the name of "Margaret" became known in many parts of the country and even abroad.

As a matter of fact, she, whose simplicity required only a few plain dresses, food, and a place to sleep was rapidly becoming a very wealthy woman. Rarely, though, did she seek recreation except through seeing her friends. Margaret's idea of a "fiesta" was a short rest in the afternoon, spent sitting in a cane-bottomed rocking chair outside the bakery. This habit, known to all who wished to seek her advice or tell her their tales of woe, resulted in an endless stream of

Seated in a rocking chair, the Bread Woman received an endless stream of visitors

visitors, who approached the benign, plump little woman as if she were royalty. It was not, however, the O'Rourke lineage that drew people to her, but a spirit of understanding and compassion, transforming the simple rocker into a throne and Margaret into a queen.

Her most frequent visitor was Louise Jarbot, who had insisted upon decorating her friend's apartment above the bakery.

"Left to your own devices," she said, "you'd be living in a whitewashed cell."

So Margaret had allowed Louise to have her way and buy appropriate pieces, designed not only for comfort but to beautify the place. She sometimes teased Louise, complaining that the frills and furbelows forced upon her as necessities, were positively smothering! Nonetheless, Margaret enjoyed her apartment, and, although she would never have taken the time for making such embellishments herself, she found beauty in the cheerful feminine décor.

One afternoon in the year 1860, when Margaret was about to retire into the house after receiving many visitors from her chair on the street, a carriage drove up. Cécile Boré alighted with her son—a three-year-old named Jacques instead of the anticipated "Margaret." They went upstairs to Margaret's living quarters, where, after the small boy delighted his listeners by reciting words recently added to his vocabulary in both English and French, Cécile said she had unhappy, startling news.

Her husband, whose family lived in Boston, had come to New Orleans only because he had inherited a small sugar refinery from his uncle. His sister Jane had joined her parents soon after graduation, made her debut in Boston, and subsequently married there. Because of the war talk, the

Adams family—whose sympathies were with the North—
had persuaded George to sell the refinery so that he could
come home.

"Of course," Cécile went on, "I have to go with George.
But the idea that he might be called upon to fight against—
against . . . Margaret, it's terrible!"

"I am still praying that war will not come," Margaret said.

"I am, too," Cécile assured her, "but every day one sees
more uniforms on the street. And it is rumored that General
Beauregard is considering leaving his post at West Point
to return to New Orleans. This must mean that the South
intends to secede from the Union. Oh, Margaret, how do you
feel about all this?"

After a moment of silence, Margaret said, "I've been
giving to these matters much thought, Cécile. And, my heart
is heavy with the idea that our country may be divided. I love
New Orleans! It has been my home and I feel loyalty for all
the blessings bestowed on me since living here. But I cannot
believe that there are not those in the North with sincerity
no less deep than our own. While I am sympathetic with
the grave problems of the South, no matter what happens I
will never be able to consider fellow Americans my enemies.
Perhaps these are not the words of a true patriot, but
America is my country, not North, South, East or West—all
of America."

"Most people do not share this view," Cécile said, "and
I can understand why Mama is beside herself. This parting
with my parents is not an ordinary one. Oh, Margaret, it is
sad—sad!"

"It is. And if war *does* come, your case will be multiplied
over and over again—families separated and fighting one
against another—"

"I must go with my husband but I can scarcely bear it," Cécile said, bursting into tears.

Frightened by her sobs, small Jacques also started to cry. At the sound of his wails, Cécile clasped the little boy in her arms.

"Mama was just being silly," she said. "Little Jacques and Mama and Papa are going to Boston for a nice long visit. We will have such fun!"

Cécile hoisted the child above her shoulder so that he could not see her face, and went on, "What I came for, Margaret, is to bid you adieu."

"Now! When are you leaving?"

"We sail tomorrow on *The Natchez*."

"So soon!"

Both women wanted to weep and embrace before parting. Instead, they gazed at one another in silence so that the child would not be frightened.

In spite of her effort, Margaret's voice was thick with sorrow when she said, "Yes, little Jacques, you'll have a lovely time—such fun."

"You will look in on Mama," Cécile whispered.

"You know I will."

"I do know, Margaret, I love you."

As little Jacques echoed her words in a childish treble, Margaret turned away. "Go, Cécile, go," she said. The child must not see her tears, but as they moved toward the door, she managed to murmur, "It will not be too long. Maybe it will not happen."

But, soon after, a young lawyer named Lincoln moved into the White House. He would be no President of the South! Jefferson Davis would head the Confederacy! Let General Pierre Gustave Toutant Beauregard come home to

New Orleans and raise an army! If the Yankees were going to tell *them* what to do, if *they* had to take orders from the Federal Government, well—like all red-blooded Southern states, Louisiana would secede!

10

A City Untamed

Along with the other states where prosperity depended upon cotton and slaves, Louisiana had left the Union. The Stars and Stripes had been hauled down to be replaced by the Stars and Bars of the Confederacy. No longer was New Orleans a city divided by petty social distinctions. A deeper cause had been carved out by history, events heralded in the headlines of the *Times-Picayune* and by travelers returning home to report Yankees on the march, towns taken, cities besieged. Yet up until now the Confederate forces were holding their own.

General Beauregard had resigned his post at West Point and returned to his beloved New Orleans. Here this most dashing Creole officer in all the Confederacy consulted with General Lovell, who was to take charge of the troops in the city. Not that the Yanks would ever get that far, for Beauregard was now at Fort Sumter and his troops were holding! Still, Southern chivalry had no meaning for Northern barbarians, so the city must be prepared.

As Margaret made her way to the Boré house, a New Orleans contingent was drilling in the Place d'Armes. It was a Zouave Company, their scarlet fezzes and baggy Moroccan trousers calling to mind dolls at drill rather than grim men ready to take their place beside comrades battling to the death.

But they were real, Margaret thought, they were real. Her sense of waiting to awaken from a nightmare and discover all was well again was wishful thinking. Yes, the nightmare was a reality and it had transformed her friend Madame Boré from a charming, happy woman into a semi-invalid.

Wan, listless, she greeted Margaret absently, as if her friend's presence had no power to lure her from the inner life into which she had withdrawn.

"I won't be asking if you have heard from Cécile," Margaret said, "because I've had no news from my brother in Baltimore. Mail will not be coming through. And, if you intend to lie around until it does, I doubt that your legs will hold you up."

Margaret had discovered that a crisp, salty attitude toward Madame Boré seemed a better weapon against her apathy than sympathetic words.

Now Madame stirred, gazing at Margaret reproachfully. "What difference does it make whether I walk or no? What difference does anything make?" she asked.

"These are questions you have to answer for yourself," Margaret told her. "I'm sure Monsieur Boré is upset by your unhappiness. Besides, in times like these, there are many people you could help."

"Me, help? I am the one who needs help."

"You do," Margaret admitted. "But unless you lend willingness to those who want to help you too, they can do nothing."

Madame Boré took refuge in silence again, and withdrew into her own thoughts. Whatever they were, they brought a soft smile to her lips.

"It is good to see you smile," Margaret told her.

". . . It was such a pleasant evening," Madame Boré said dreamily. "The most beautiful opera—Adelina Patti never sang better—*Lucia di Lammermoor*. Such beautiful gowns and jewels and fans—and only a year ago." She was silent for a moment, then went on softly, "Cécile was the most beautiful young matron in the house. Every eye was turned in the direction of our box. She could have had her pick of aristocracy, but no. Instead, it had to be George, with his New England airs, his Harvard education." Bitterness tinged her tones as this small tirade ended.

"I thought you'd become very fond of George," Margaret said.

Madame Boré burst into tears. "I had," she wailed, "but he has taken Cécile away to side with the enemy. What would you have me do, Margaret? Help make bullets that might kill the Yankee father of my grandchild?"

"No," Margaret said. "There are other ways to help. The women of the city have organized into groups for many services. To learn nursing, to visit those who have lost their sons, help comfort the sick and other acts prompted by the heart to aid humanity. Louise Jarbot is instructing a group in nursing, and I thought perhaps you might be interested."

"I am too ill," Madame Boré protested.

"Perhaps you are," Margaret said. "Nonetheless, I will leave a schedule of her classes with you. Maybe you might change your mind. We'll need all the help we can get."

"I'll think about it," Madame Boré said.

Since this was more than Margaret had expected, she went away satisfied.

Back at the bakery, she attended to various tasks associated with her business. Orders had to be filled, and a new appraisal made of earnings and expenses. Gold and silver were disappearing from the market and Confederate paper tender was the chief medium of exchange. The state of Louisiana had one paper issue, the city another. There was also a flood of "shin-plasters" or "money" issued by certain merchants, which in normal times would have been completely valueless. Although essential commodities had risen sky-high, Margaret tried to keep the price of her confections down even when she was forced to pay more for the ingredients. Longer and longer grew the lists of patrons who could not pay at all, but the needy must have their "daily bread" if she could manage.

When, because of the recession, lines of the unemployed grew longer, Margaret opened a small coffee shop where drifters and those unfit for service could stave off hunger with a steaming cup of soup, coffee and products from her bakery. With food sold practically at cost, this place became the rendezvous for beggars, misfits and lowly characters who roamed the waterfront.

For those whose slurred speech and unsteady gait suggested frequent visits to the tavern, Margaret had a method by which her alms would find a place as part of the family meal. For she had learned that often a loaf of bread was sold before it reached the home, in order to obtain a shot of whiskey. So, if a beggar was suspect, she'd neatly slice the loaf in half, assuring against its salability. She often chatted with these impoverished patrons, many of whom told of what had brought them to their present lowly state.

There was one young man who came often to the coffee shop; unlike many of the others he had an air of respectability and seemed drawn there by preference rather than need. He always had money to pay for his food, his clothes were well brushed, his shoes shined, and he carried himself with an air of dignity. In her talks with him, Margaret learned that he was but recently out of work because his previous employer had been forced to shut down, owing to lack of shipping. Other merchandise had made way for essential war material, and the wooden ships on the upper Mississippi were spiked with cannon. Timorous was the traveler who roamed the river now, and nonessential trade had slowed down to a trickle.

Margaret was drawn to this young man, who in some strange way reminded her of her husband Charles. His name was Bernard Klotz, and he eagerly sought work until that time when he might be accepted into the Southern armies. Meanwhile, Margaret offered him a job in the bakery, and this proved a boon to them both. Initiative and imagination made Klotz an invaluable consultant in all phases of the enterprise. His winning personality proved a great advantage to customer relations, and his youth bolstered Margaret's daring to expand and improvise. Soon, her bakery was seething with the new sounds of machinery operated by overhead pulleys and belts, powered by a steam engine. First in her wholehearted generosity to the poor, she now owned the first "steam bakery" in the South. Besides, she had an able young helper who could supervise when her presence was demanded by pressing duties of the time.

Much to Margaret's joy, Madame Boré did decide to attend the courses in nursing, and the knowledge that she was needed again gave meaning to her life.

Months wore on, and crowds daily gathered around "Newspaper Row" along Camp Street. Journalism in New Orleans during that century was enriched by such names as Mark Twain and Walt Whitman, whose writings raised the tone of newspaper columns to heights of literature. Now, however, it was news, unembellished and stark, that caused the populace to approach the printed sheet with grave anxiety.

It says in *The Times-Picaytme*, it says in *The Gazette*, that the Federal Navy intends to blockade the Gulf ports. Wait, though, until those Yanks get a pounding from Forts Jackson and St. Philip! Still, *The Picayune* says General Lovell is evacuating all troops from the city, in the event—though it is highly improbable—that the forts fall to the enemy. Lovell also left orders, that should there be a break-through, everything must be burned which would help the cause of the cursed Yanks. But this could not happen—Farragut's fleet would be battered to bits!

So, those swarming around Newspaper Row picked up the air of one who had whistled, and they, too, whistled, hummed or sang:

> *I wish I was in de land of cotton, cinnamon seed and sandy*
> *bottom, Look a-way*
> *A-way in Dix-ey*
> *Dix-ey's land where I was born on one frosty morning,*
> *Look a-way*
> *A-way in Dix-ey.* . . .

Whistle, sing, hum small tunes of defiance, yet gradually the headlines stood too bold for pretense. All one could do was wait.

March, 1862: SHIP ISLAND OCCUPIED BY FEDS. Ship

Island, that white sandy wasteland, which had once been a gala summer resort, rendezvous for the fashionable until their homes were literally washed away during a hurricane! April 18, 1862: FARRAGUT'S FLEET BOMBARDING FORTS JACKSON AND ST. PHILIP. This headline was followed by news that Brigadier General Duncan had reported to General Lovell that even if heavy bombardment continued through the night, his men could stand it as long as the Yanks. He added, "Our barbet guns are still in working order. . . . The health of the troops continues good. ... We are still cheerful, and have an abiding faith in our ultimate success."

For the following five days, news was sparse, but New Orleans was confident that the Confederate forts would hold and the enemy ships would be driven back.

The night of April 24, Margaret slept fitfully. Over and over, it seemed, she dreamed that a large oven of bread had caught fire, the shiny brown loaves charred to black tissue. Then, came the sound of knocking at her door, insistent, continuous—that was not a dream. Fully awakened, her eyes smarted from smoke. At first Margaret thought the building was on fire, and someone had come to summon her. She threw open the door for Chloe, who announced in frightened tones that one of the Sisters was waiting and wished to see her at once.

"The smoke—" Margaret said uncertainly.

"Yes," her maid replied. "Smoke is everywhere."

As Margaret hurried down the stairs, she saw in the misty gray of the night outside orange streaks shooting up from the waterfront.

"Is the city on fire, Miss Margaret?" Chloe asked.

Not the city, no. But bales of tobacco, cotton and heaven knew what, being put to the torch so as not to be seized by the enemy. New Orleans was perhaps in a state of siege, Margaret thought. Was this, then, why the nun had come, perhaps thinking the city itself would be razed?

In the dim light of a lantern, Sister Emily's starched white cornette appeared.

"Margaret!" Sister's voice betrayed deep emotion, but it did not seem to stem from fear.

Seeking to comfort her, Margaret said, "Though the situation does seem bad, I can't believe the city will be bombarded. There's no reason—we are practically without troops, without defences."

Softly weeping, the nun replied, "It is not this, Margaret. It is Sister Regis."

Shoulders shaking with sobs, she could not go on.

"What about Sister Regis? Is she ill?"

When the nun still did not speak, but only shook her head, Margaret knew. Sister Regis was dead.

"When? How? Why did they not tell me of her illness?"

"There was no illness. Sister passed away quietly in her sleep."

The room was suddenly lit by orange pinnacles traced against the wall, and there came the low rumble of an explosion on the wharves. Probably some kegs of alcohol or metal bands snapping off bales of cotton. But the bizarre wavering reflections went unnoticed. Margaret was stunned by the news of her loss. Her friend, Sister Regis, dead!

Now heat from flames on the levee nearby could be felt in the room. Chloe came in.

"The fire is getting awful close, Miss Margaret," she said. "I hopes the wind doesn't blow this way."

The bell on St. Patrick's was still pealing a summons to members of the volunteer fire company.

"I don't think it will spread," Margaret told her maid.

"Anyhow, you'd be given warning, Chloe. Now I must dress and go along with Sister Emily."

When they reached St. Therese's Asylum, it seemed incredible, unreal that her dear friend was not among those present. Yet lowered heads, eyes reddened from weeping, set a seal of truth upon the fact that Sister Regis was gone, and would not return again.

Because of uncertainty about the city—whether it might be bombarded or merely occupied—Sister Regis was buried within the next few days. Margaret paid for her vault, saying that when she died it was her wish to be placed alongside one who had been truly in spirit her sister as well as her most beloved friend.

After the requiem Mass, when the cortege was returning, Margaret saw crowds of people hurrying toward the St. Charles Hotel. She would go there, too. Sorrow for Sister Regis' passing would remain until her own life was done, but now she was needed, all were' needed! What present crisis was drawing the citizens of New Orleans toward the St. Charles Hotel like bits of steel to a magnet?

Margaret learned that during the night General Benjamin Butler of the Federal armies had entered the city. He and his troops were billeted at the St. Charles Hotel, where the General was now in consultation with the Mayor of New Orleans concerning measures for the occupation of the city. That they could be making much headway with the din going on outside seemed highly improbable. The mob spilled far beyond the confines of the hotel, with heckling, catcalls, and threats directed toward a balcony; in the room beyond, it had been reported, the two men were in conference.

One of the hotel waiters who had joined the mob gleefully

told how the manager had warned one of General Butler's officers against bringing his troops into the hotel.

"Said the General might find poison in his fish."

Here, the waiter elbowed sidewise, not caring whose ribs received the jab. They were Margaret's.

"Mind your manners and your tongue," she said a trifle sharply. "Irresponsible talk of poison and the like will only make more misery."

"Oh, pardon me, Miss Margaret! But Yank soldiers are swarming all over the city; they've taken the Custom House. You wouldn't want to just let it go at that, would you?

"It's little choice we've got," Margaret said, "with the Federal fleet close by and ready to bombard the city at a given order."

A curtain stirred and the Mayor stepped out onto the balcony. His face was white; he held up his hands for silence.

"Please listen to me," he pleaded. "General Butler—"

He was interrupted by boos.

"Listen! General Butler says, if you do not disband, he will find an unpleasant way to clear the streets."

"Let him try!" shouted a man named Mumford. "Let him come out and see what we think of him and his—Yankee flag!"

Here, the misguided young man pointed to his lapel, where a shredded strip of the Stars and Stripes formed a boutonniere. He and some other young blades had hauled down a Union flag, dragged it through the street, then tore it up to wear as a symbol of their defiance.

The mob took up the cry. "Where's Old Butler? Let him show himself; let him come out here if he dares!"

Suddenly, then, the lace curtain parted and General Butler stood alongside the Mayor. The latter promptly turned on his heel and left the balcony.

"Who calls me?" Butler asked. "I am here."

Lean, keen-eyed and with not a trace of fear on his face, Butler surveyed the crowd. His gaze lingered a trifle long on the man Mumford, eyes seeming to bore a hole directly into the shredded bit of flag, which, to the General, symbolized an act of desecration. There, at that moment, he decided young Mumford would be hanged.

Though this verdict was later to be challenged by men in high places, Butler's deficiency as a diplomat prevented him from altering a course once he had adopted it. This lack, more than any great evil in the man, caused him to be called "Beast Butler" by the people of New Orleans during the two-year occupation by Federal troops.

Now, though, silence had fallen upon the gathering, shoulder pressed close against shoulder, defying intention to move.

Suddenly, then, the Sixth Maine Battery, commanded by Captain Thompson, dashed full-speed down St. Charles Street. Over the uneven, foot-square granite blocks, Thompson rode, with cannoneers clinging to their seats, and the wheels of the guns thundering on the rough paving.

As the mob scattered, some, at least, must have had at least a premonition that General Butler's intentions would be carried out. Nonetheless, there continued on every side efforts to defy him.

When a stench spread over the city, and the General demanded that canals and waterways be cleansed, he was told in all innocence that this was never done. Resentment had reached a point where citizens preferred risking an epidemic of yellow fever—since such a scourge would first take off the rose-cheeked Yankees —to removing the source

With not a trace of fear on his face, General Butler surveyed the crowd

of pollution. Thus, General Butler was forced to use his own staff of engineers and soldiers to dredge and drain possible areas of contamination.

The women of New Orleans were especially troublesome. Soldiers from the North, fearful of the plague and homesick, craved a friendly word, a comforting smile from women who reminded them of the wives, mothers, sweethearts left behind. Knowing this, the ladies of New Orleans, on encountering Yankee soldiers on the street, would first smile, as if they intended friendliness, then when a Bluecoat came close, they performed an act which ordinarily would have been seriously frowned upon. They spat on enemy uniforms, then, with a swish of their skirts, moved haughtily away!

Butler, a good general and an excellent administrator, managed to feed the populace, and insisted that all welfare agencies be maintained. Devotion to duty was his avowed virtue, and this he tried to exemplify by his behavior. But, lacking imagination, the General was recurrently amazed that duty and discipline gained him few admirers.

Anxious to meet with key people in the community, Butler asked for an interview with Margaret and Father Mullon. When they arrived at the General's personal quarters in the St. Charles, he made every effort to cast upon the conference a tone of camaraderie. However, what he considered warmth was a trickle of ice against the spine.

"Miss Margaret," he said, "your work with the soldiers has been most gratifying. Your foresight in including generosity to both sides I have rewarded by permitting you to continue the purchase of flour."

"That you have," Margaret agreed, "but it's many a hassle I've had with your pickets to let me through the lines."

"This," the General said, "was before I was convinced that

you and your women's committees were bent on missions of mercy. Treatment of my troops by Southern 'ladies' often made me wonder if the female of New Orleans was worthy of that name."

"If you will pardon me, General," Margaret replied, "it seems to me that your way of banding people together under a single head doesn't do you credit."

"I am a general, not a Creole dilettante," was the brusque reply.

Butler then turned to Father Mullon.

"And, you, Father," he said, "have caused me much perplexity. As a man of God, I should imagine the cause against slavery would be your own. Instead you have been hostile to me since my arrival, pitted your wits against mine and surreptitiously prayed for Confederate successes."

"Some of your points are well taken," Father Mullon said. "But I do not espouse slavery; indeed, selling human beings has always been abhorrent to me. This system, though, has parallel in the North with bigotry, Nativism, underpaid child labor and offenses too numerous to mention. Now, don't misunderstand, General. Two wrongs do not make a right, nor do I wish to give this as an impression. But I warn you, sir, to overhasten the matter of abolishing slavery will result only in another form of the exploitation of those who have been freed.

"You may not know it, General, but most of our people care for their slaves as if they were members of the family, deeming it their duty to provide for the welfare of those who loyally serve them. This, though, has not been my quarrel with you, sir. But when any man threatens to remove the bells on churches to fashion them into bullets, this I cannot abide. You have already, sir, all of the gold and silversmiths in the city making armaments; is this, sir, not enough?"

"I did recall the order about church bells," General Butler said.

"And wisely so," Father Mullon put in, "because even among your own men, such an act would have rebounded with disfavor."

Butler's face was thoughtful. Indeed, he had the puzzled look of a man, who, now desiring respect, was met only with hostility.

"Besides," Father Mullon went on, "you mentioned 'surreptitious prayers.' No. The prayers of all are for an end to hostilities. But if in their hearts the Southerner feels wronged by intruders who have laid waste their land and started a bloodbath between brothers, I fully share this emotion. Each prays according to his own conscience. This cannot be regulated by your excessive and ruthless proclamations."

Now angry, the General said, "Since you insist upon insubordination, let us be more specific about my request for this meeting, Father. It has come to my attention that you have refused burial services for some of the Federal soldiers."

Father Mullon shook his head. "You should realize the falsity of this rumor," he said evenly. Then he smiled. "Because figuratively speaking, sir, I should like nothing better than to bury the *whole* Federal army." The twinkle in his eye was lost upon the General, who now gravely turned to Margaret. "And, you, Margaret, it has been reported that you physically pushed aside a picket guarding Southern prisoners. What is your answer to this?"

"My answer is 'guilty,' " she replied. "And I've pushed aside pickets guarding Northern hospitals too. When men are suffering and require a bit of nursing, hungry and yearning for decent food, no upstart picket will keep me from passing.

You may tell them, General, to stop me with their bayonets!"
Curiously, then, the General said wearily, "I will give them orders to always let you pass."

After two years of occupying New Orleans, General Benjamin Butler included these words in his farewell address:

> "Citizens of New Orleans, it may not be inappropriate, as it is not inopportune an occasion, that there should be addressed to you a few words of parting, by one whose name is hereafter indissolubly connected with your city.

> "I shall speak in no bitterness, because I am not conscious of a single personal animosity. Commanding the Army of the Gulf, I have found you captured, but not surrendered; conquered but not orderly; relieved from the presence of an army but incapable of taking care of yourselves. I restored order, punished crime, opened commerce, brought provisions to your starving people, reformed your currency, and gave you quiet protection, such as you have not enjoyed for many years.

> "While doing this, my soldiers were subjected to obloquy, reproach, and insult.

> "I am speaking the farewell words of one who has shown his devotion to his country at the peril of his life and fortune, who in these words can have neither hope nor interest, save the good of those whom he addresses; and let me here repeat with all solemnity of an appeal to Heaven to bear me witness, that such are the views forced upon me by experience.

"Come, then, to the unconditional support of the Government, take into your own hands your institutions', remodel them according to the laws of the Nation and of God, and thus attain the great prosperity assured to you by geographical position, only a portion of which was heretofore yours."

Though Margaret never admitted it aloud, she felt Butler did not deserve the name of "Beast." He, too, acted according to his conscience, and in this light faithfully performed his duty.

11

OUR PEOPLE

It was strange, Margaret thought, that a panorama of the past could seem far more real than happenings in the present. This was not so when visitors came, but the doctor had given orders they should be limited.

"Otherwise," he said, "the room will have the appearance of a reception hall. And, Margaret, it is better for you to conserve your strength. You know you have been ill."

Margaret knew, not only that she *had* been, but that she still was ill. Otherwise, she would not now be a patient in the Hôtel Dieu, which was in truth a hospital. She had been there for quite a while, and though her friends, the doctor and nurses, spoke of a rosy future, she did not believe them. Nonetheless, when Louise came to call and said, "When you get out of here, you'll come to live with me," Margaret smiled and told her, "Yes, of course, I will." She did not believe it, however, and doubted that the others expected her ever to leave the Hôtel Dieu. But if it made them happy to pretend— she would pretend too.

Chief conspirator in concealment was Sister Irene, whose devoted nursing was heightened by their bond of secrecy.

"Promise me, Sister," Margaret would say, "you'll not tell my friends about the pains I had last night."

"I promise."

Those pains passed as had the others, and Margaret still managed to move around her room, sit in a chair to receive visitors, or, when too fatigued, lie in bed, thoughts drifting to the past.

It was a sunny afternoon in 1882. She'd already had one visitor, a young woman from St. Elizabeth's Industrial School, one of Margaret's pet projects. From personal experience, she had learned of the disappointments experienced by untrained women when seeking satisfactory employment. St. Elizabeth's fitted them for the kind of work best suited to their abilities.

Margaret sat in a large armchair near a window where the sun streamed in to highlight a gift, an exquisitely stitched "wrapper" draped across her knees. Of navy blue, lightweight wool, the collar was embroidered with delicate sprays of forget-me-nots. Now, one of the most sought-after seamstresses in New Orleans, this young woman had learned her trade at St. Elizabeth's. As Margaret softly stroked a clump of raised flowers, she gave a sigh of satisfaction.

Sister Irene came bustling into the room, the points of her cornette quivering with disapproval. "Back to bed with you, now, Margaret," she scolded. "You must rest for at least an hour. Another visitor is scheduled for this evening."

Here, Sister caught sight of the lovely wrapper. "Well," she said, "if you aren't going to be the debutante!" And she chatted on about how Margaret would bedazzle her guests with such finery, adding the warning, "But if you don't take a rest, you'll see no one else."

Grateful Margaret was for clean-smelling pillows and sheets where she could stretch her weary body. She had to admit that each day brought longer spans of weakness, intervals when what she wanted most was to lie in bed and let her thoughts linger upon the past. After Sister lowered the shade, she gazed about, marveling at the generosity of others. Her room was never without flowers from friends, acquaintances, and even strangers claiming cause for gratitude to her. And, heavenly Saints! Her hand moved toward a table close beside her bed, fingers tracing the outline of a crucifix. Father Hubert had brought it the day before. Imagine, all the way from Rome, a gift to her from the Pope! You'd think the Holy Father would have enough to do without bothering about the likes of me!

During the past week, her plunges into the past mostly brought up memories of those who had died. Somehow, though, sorrow for their loss seemed lacking—indeed, she felt as if they would soon be clasping hands.

. . . Father Mullon. The good man had gone not long after Sister Regis, both being spared those terrible days of Reconstruction when New Orleans had been overrun by adventurers—carpetbagger Northern rogues who got control of the government. Those were sad times for both Negroes and whites, with ex-slaves who had previously toiled in the field now holding high offices.

But what about the other poor blacks? Promised by Republicans "a mule and forty acres," they'd roamed the South, pitiful beggars, many seeking their old masters for protection. Some of her own slaves had returned, and Jackson, faithful Jackson, still worked at her bakery. It was not her own bakery alone now, because when she'd felt her health failing, it seemed only sensible to incorporate the enterprise, giving her adopted son, Bernard Klotz, the largest share of stock.

Father Mullon. . . . What would he have thought of the "White League" battling against Negroes and carpetbaggers in the streets of New Orleans? Those had been terrible years. Wide funnel-stacked engines luring trade from the river—the South, a brutally beaten stepchild of the Union, indeed only recently restored to partial favor.

But most of all—here, Margaret felt her lips drawing upward into a smile—what would that gallant Confederate priest and gentleman have said when she, Margaret Haughery, had presented a gold jeweled sword to a Yankee general? But the war was over then, and wounds had started to heal.

Time tilted back to that period. It was 1877, and General Beauregard, favorite son of New Orleans, could now be openly honored as a wartime hero—and to none was more homage paid. Imagine! One day when she, Margaret Haughery, Bread Woman of New Orleans, was seated on her cane chair outside the bakery, the dashing general alighted from his carriage. She'd invited him in, and after hastily tidying up a bit, they'd sat there drinking *café-au-lait* and eating French bread, warm from the oven. After praising her for all the good work she'd done, and she accusing the General of blarney, he told her of having come there for a special reason. It seemed that General Augur, who had been in command of the Department of the Gulf, was being retired from that post which was no longer needed.

"As Yankees go," General Beauregard said, "he has exhibited astonishing virtues and asks, as a reward, to meet you, Margaret."

"General Augur is a gentleman," she replied, "and has done much to erase bitterness caused by the dreadful war. Besides, it's a pretty humble character he must be, counting it a reward to meet the likes of myself. I would be honored to have a small reception for him —nothing formal—right here in my place. If you would be so good as to arrange it, and let me know the date."

The General said he would.

Margaret remembered how the gathering had symbolized hope that this great and glorious country would never again be divided by strife. She had counted such an occasion worthy of a gift to a man whose consideration for the people of New Orleans had done much to dim the image of "Yankee barbarian." She saw herself again in the beautiful jewelry store of Griswold & Company ordering the sword. She recalled her agitation lest it might not arrive on time. But it had—a beautiful golden sword set with jewels. The Boré's were there, including Cécile and her husband. More beautiful than ever, Cécile looked like a sister to her sixteen-year-old daughter Margaret.

On her pillow, now, the old Margaret smiled and murmured, "My dear godchild."

It had been a grand reception—and General Augur had written her a lovely letter:

> *"My Good Friend Margaret: ... It is very gratifying to me that you should have found anything good connected with the performance of my Military duties in accordance with your views of life, as to have induced the presentation of so valuable a gift.*

General Augur accepted the golden sword

I can assure you, very truthfully, there are but few persons from whom I could have accepted it, but from you who have, for the greater part of your life, devoted yourself and the abundant fruit of your labors entirely to the destitute orphans and poor of New Orleans, and whose name is never mentioned except with the greatest respect and affection, I esteem it a great honor to receive this evidence of your regard.

I have many children, and the sword, with the "story of Margaret" will be preserved among them, with pride, as long as they and their descendants live. . .

"I have many children—I have—"

Margaret's eyelids drooped and she feel asleep.

After her dinner, Sister Irene draped the new wrapper around Margaret's shoulders and helped her to the chair.

"Who is my visitor this evening?" Margaret asked.

Sister always played a little game of "surprise," withholding identity of the expected guest.

"This is an old friend," she said. "You have not seen him for quite a while."

"Who?"

"I think I'll let the gentleman announce himself," Sister Irene said, then she left the room.

There was a timid knock on the door, and, when he first stepped in, Margaret did not recognize her guest. He smiled, and— Only on one face had she ever seen such a gentle smile, heard so much compassion in a voice, as when he said, "How are you, Miss Margaret?"

"Thomy Lafon!"

"Yes, Miss Margaret, I've been stopping most every day to ask about your health, and Sister suggested I come in."

"But why didn't you ask? There's none I'd rather see."

"I feared to tire you," Thomy Lafon said.

They spoke of the first time they'd met, and of many events that had happened since.

Presently he said, "I won't stay long, Miss Margaret. You must not tax your strength."

"A little longer," she begged.

"As I predicted," Thomy Lafon said, "my people are now free. With more education, they're beginning to recognize their true friends. You, Miss Margaret, you—" Thomy's eyes filled with tears. "I think I'd better be going, Miss Margaret."

As he turned to leave, Margaret said, "Wait! You wouldn't go without shaking my hand."

Their hands clasped and Thomy Lafon left.

Quickly, so Sister could not prevent her, Margaret knelt beside her bed. "*Our* Father who art in Heaven . . ."

Not *my* Father, not *your* Father, but *OUR* Father. Peace, love. . . . Not North, South, East or West, but please someday, dear Father, all the world.

Margaret felt weak, she was shaking, and suddenly there seemed a warm cloak spreading over her shoulders. The cloak—she would wear—in—the—future. . . .

Dimly, she heard Sister Irene say, "Send for Father Hubert at once. Get the doctor quickly, quickly."

In the procession that bore Margaret to her tomb next to Sister Regis were two Louisiana governors, the Mayor of New Orleans, representatives of the Chamber of Commerce, eleven groups of orphans.

Except for bequests to her adopted son, Bernard Klotz, to Louise Jarbot and to her maid Clothilde, all Margaret's fabulous fortune was bequeathed to the poor of New Orleans—of every age, creed and color.

In the French Quarter, on a triangular plot, stands the statue of a woman carved in Carrara marble. Pennies, dimes, dollars were voluntarily given so that passers-by could see the likeness of this woman, seated in her cane chair, with two children beside her. Although the traditional shawl is draped around her shoulders, there is another, more visible in her many acts of love. Transformed is the humble shawl into a shiny warm cloak, to be worn forever and ever—and ever.

Margaret Haughery

Author's Note

All historical events and those concerning Margaret Haughery's life are true. Due to the lack of specific mention of names making up her everyday existence, Minna Weber, the Boré family, Patrick Murphy, Paul, and Jackson have been invented. All other characters are actual, living in New Orleans at the same time as Margaret.

Most of the biographical data on Margaret Haughery was supplied by Sister M. Catharine Joseph, I.H.M., of Immaculata College, Immaculata, Pennsylvania, to whom I am indebted for her extensive and painstaking research. Helping to round out the picture of Margaret was a pamphlet published by the Klotz Bakery, entitled *M. H.* For background material on New Orleans and the events in that city during the 19th century, my major sources were *New Orleans*, by Oliver Evans (The Macmillan Company, New York, 1959); *New Orleans City Guide*, revised by Robert Tallant (Houghton Mifflin Company, Boston, 1952); and *Fabulous New Orleans*, by Lyle Saxon (D. Ap- pleton-Century Company, New York, 1939).

F.S.